T0381436

THE
Meaning
OF
God

Love Explained on
Rumi's Poetry

DORIS KESSLER

Balboa Press books may be ordered through booksellers or by contacting:

Balboa Press
A Division of Hay House
1663 Liberty Drive
Bloomington, IN 47403
www.balboapress.com
1 (877) 407-4847

ISBN: 978-1-9822-3527-7 (sc)
ISBN: 978-1-9822-3526-0 (e)

Library of Congress Control Number: 2019914492

Print information available on the last page.

Balboa Press rev. date: 11/14/2019

BALBOA.
PRESS
A DIVISION OF HAY HOUSE

Table of Contents

Preface

This book is written in honor of infinite Source that nourishes every single one of us and all parts of creation with it's beautiful unconditional Love and Light. This book is also in honor of Rumi, one of my greatest teachers in getting to know God, what it is, where it can be found, and how we connect to it.

I chose to write this book in order to empower every human being on this planet, because *"my religion is Love, and every heart is my temple" (Rumi),* and every heart is precious, no matter where or who you are.

This book is intended to empower and assist everyone looking for the truth of Life and Love, to find the connection to their divine Self, so that you can see it in everyone and everything else, too. This book is in no way intended to offend, insult, or hurt the feelings of religious people, or anyone who does not feel the same way. It is in no way intended to offend or insult any religion or religious or non-religious beliefs. The words written in this book came out of the desire of the author to share "where the light entered her wound", and do therefore reflect the feelings and thoughts of the author and are a recollection of her memories, feelings, and channelings. The reason I was inspired to write it was and is that I have observed so much suffering on this planet in many incarnations, and in my opinion, most of the suffering stemmed from a perceived illusion of being disconnected or separated from God our Source – unconditional Love, or Life, because of cultural, worldly, or religious beliefs that were not necessarily guiding humans towards the light or telling the truth, but were rather a reflection of where those 'in power' (higher in the hierarchy, since in the eyes of Source we are all equally powerful) were on their own journey towards connection back to God and Life. My only intention for this book and all to follow on this subject is to help humanity remember who we truly are - *Love*, no matter if you are religious or not, and living from that Source to create together a planet that we love, that is healthy and thriving, and humanity living in oneness instead of separation. There is nothing that God is not, for we are all an individual expression and extension of it.

Introduction

All my Life I have been living with a deep longing for connection to something I didn't know what it was. For the most of time I thought I would feel it when I finally found my man, my soul mate, my twin flame, here on Earth. But my curiosity for the ultimate truth about who we are, and why we are here, was still not satisfied when I met my ex-husband. There was something else out there that was longing to connect with me as much as I was longing to connect with it.

"What you seek is seeking you!" Rumi

I was sure that this something – I call it God or Source - would heal all my heavy-feeling emotions: sorrow, fear, sadness, grieve, anger, powerlessness, despair, disappointment, and frustration... the list goes on and on.

So I often asked the same question: Who am I? What is my origin? Where do I come from? I knew that – even though I love mother Earth and her amazing beauty dearly – I wasn't from here, this was not my origin, and that somehow I was here as a guest, a visitor. I grew up in a family where religion was not a big thing, probably also because Eastern Germany did not really promote religion; they rather wanted the people to be following the socialistic/communistic rules.

My dad came from a protestant family, and he sometimes went to church with us at Christmas, while Santa Claus (my beloved mom) turned our home into a Christmas miracle.

However, whenever I was in a church or heard the words of priests, something inside of me was unable to find a connection there, since the atmosphere was patriarchal, heavy, dark, and judgmental with the pictures of a suffering Jesus on the walls. I did not find nor could I feel Love there, and the idea that Jesus was God seemed somewhat limited to me, in fact, he himself called himself a 'son of God'. Somehow the idea that one human being was God seemed too small to me, for I felt that God could not be reduced or limited to only one human being. So, what or where was God, and where would I find it?

Gandhi once said: "Where there is Love, there is Life." When I think of my upbringing, I don't remember much life during my childhood, for I experienced much tension at home. I grew up in a little beautiful 1000-year-old town in Eastern Germany. The German culture – at least when I was little – did not promote much affection. I remember that my mother kissed us good night, but I can't remember she ever hugged me when I was little, and to this day, I can feel that she seems somehow uncomfortable when I hug her. I've experienced only little affection as a child, and if so, mainly from my Grand-Grandma. I also never heard the words "I love you". It was a dictated schedule of breakfast, school, lunch in school, school, homework, dinner with my parents and sisters, and only little time to play or doing what I loved, which was drawing, listening to music, or being out in nature, dwelling in it's miracles and forgetting the world around me.

Earlier in my years, when I went to Kindergarden, my two other sisters were with my father's mom, who took care of them, while I loved spending time with my Grand-Grandmother, the mother of my mother's father. I called her Beppo-Oma, for she had a bird once that was called Beppo. I was lucky and happy to spend time with her, since she gave me much of what all children need the most: Love, plenty of Affection, and praise when I did well what I loved - drawing. I remember our cuddle times dearly. Early in the morning, my mom took her 3 girls on her bike – she had a basket in the front and on the rear of her bike, and I remember how much I loved sitting in one of these baskets. My mom would drop off my sisters at my Dad's mom, while I was dropped off at 'Beppo-Oma's' home, and then my mother left for work. She was a nurse, and when she finished her shifts, she would always come back to pick us up. I loved this time outside on the bike with my mother. Whenever I arrived at Beppo-Oma's home in the morning, we went straight back to bed, and she held me in her arms and her warm energy. I felt safe there. I felt like she saw 'me', and who I was, and made me draw portraits or animals or landscapes, and then I got rewarded with a wonderful and simple chocolate sand cake that I loved. I loved her dearly and I am forever grateful for her presence in my life.

Then, I started school at 6, they called me pre-mature, and my most beautiful time of the day was the time to walk to school, smelling the fresh morning air, feeling the Earth still quiet and waking up to a new day, the flower blossoms along the way just opening in spring and summer time, the energy sleepy yet excited. My walk back from school was livelier, it was usually 3 or 4 in the afternoon, and the energy did not longer seem fresh and pure, like in the mornings.

I often wondered on my way back from school: Why do I have to learn all this non-sense? What will it serve me? Yes, I sure loved writing, for it was art to me, yet all the other subjects that were kind of preferred like math or physics, were not inspiring to me and I felt bored. I wanted to learn about the cycles of the moon and nature; I wanted to get to know the stars that I saw each night, and the connection between humanity and the planets, I wanted to learn, or rather *remember*, how to live happily, light and joyful. My child's eyes saw the beauty of nature in every blossom, every grass, every tree, every cloud, every bit of blue sky above me - and blue sky was rather rare and kind of reserved for summer where I grew up, and the school curriculum seemed not in alignment with what nature taught me.

The time I enjoyed the most back in my early teenage years was my time with 'Daddy', a little brown Pekinese dog that I started walking after school for a neighbor. I impatiently waited for the neighbor to come home so that I could finally take my little furry friend, who was a bundle of love and joy, into my arms and walk with him through our beloved nature grounds. His boundless, infinite and unconditional love and joy intrigued me… I felt like he reminded me of something that was within myself, too… Today I can say that this little 4-legged friend of mine was one of my greatest teachers.

There was a little playground behind our apartment house, and I loved watching the leaves of trees changing with the 4 seasons. I realized that some trees had a similar form like their leaves. I felt the strength of trees, and they gave me strength. I loved the scent of the blossoms of a tree; with the apple tree blossoms smelling like freshly washed linen, the pear blossoms a bit like liver and tart, and the cherry blossoms very sweet and gentle. I believe this was the time, maybe 5 – 6 years old, when I wanted to smell every flower I saw. And still to this day, I would stop and smell a flower when I walk by. The scent of flowers reminded me of a truth somewhere deeply hidden… Someone once said 'stop and look at a flower, smell her scent and see her beauty, and in this scent and her beauty you will find God.' I did not know this back then, but I remember I loved flowers of all kinds, especially roses and lilac, and I would always stop and admire the beauty of the flowers when I walked by.

Often on weekends, we would either go to our garden in the countryside, or we would go see my Grandparents (my mother's parents and her brother and family) in the countryside. We had a little bungalow in a forest nearby, maybe 20 car minutes away, where my mom grew veggies and where there were fruit trees, the pride of my dad. We had apple, cherry, and pear trees. This was where I could be and melt into one with nature, my soothing beloved mother Earth.

When we visited my mom's parents on some weekends, my favorite time there was – other than the home-baked "Quarkspitzen" (sort of a rich pan cake) of my Grandma – my time out in nature alone with their dogs (my Grandpa had several German shepherds, Carmen, Antje, and the last one I remember was Rex), when everyone else was inside or sitting at the big family table outside in summer time. My mothers brother smoked cigarettes, and soon I remember to run away from this aggressive smell, and thus from the table, once I had finished eating. Instead, I sat with the dogs, where the air smelled good, and caressed them, and they offered me their love so gently and unconditionally. I sat with blooming cherry trees and daisies, admiring their beautiful smile and light. I saw how busy and friendly the bees were pollinating all the little wild flowers on the ground, or the blossoms on trees.

My Grandma had a little pond with frogs and fish in it. I often sat there and watched them gliding gracefully through the water, naturally going with the gentle flow of the water. All this seemed miraculous to me, and it soothed my soul. Somehow I could feel a deep sense of divine order in that beauty and rhythms of nature that I saw, heard and felt, a loving life force behind what changed the trees from having buds to flowers, then leaves, then fruit… I could also feel a deep sense of happiness and peace in nature, and I felt part of it while I was in it, and not inside a 'box', a house.

I did not experience the same ease and comfort with humankind though – where too often I experienced judgment and criticism, fear and anger, and other energies. I picked up on how people felt around me, and when I talked to someone who's dominant vibration was anger or judgment, I often thought it was me who caused it in the other, and I felt in a way guilty. However, my soul must have known that the feelings of others had nothing to do with me, because somehow I was able to survive. Today I know that the feelings shown or expressed from others towards me were only an expression of the people themselves and had nothing to do with me, even though as a child, I did not know that, and so I felt mostly uncomfortable being around people, except those that were smiling and joyful. And of course, my Grand-Grandmother had a balanced and peaceful energy in which I felt comfortable and safe.

I remember I did not want to stay with Kessler Oma, I did not feel comfortable in her energy (bless her beautiful soul though, I can only imagine what she has been through giving birth under attack during the war… maybe her only way to survive this trauma was to shut down from her feelings and emotions). Once I picked a beautiful little bunch of daisies in the fields of the Kindergarden for her and gave it to her on our way to her home, she lived about 10 walking minutes away from Kindergarden. She seemed indifferent about this gesture, and carried my little bouquet for about a minute, but then let it fall onto this busy pedestrian way where people would step on it. When I saw that, my heart cringed and I started crying, picking up as many of the little daisies that I could get before people stepped on them on their busy run. I felt sorry for the beautiful flowers that wanted to bring joy, but were ignored and not appreciated…

Today I know that this is how I felt. I thought something about me was beautiful and special and unique, but it was ignored and not appreciated, nobody could really 'see' it, and thus they could not see me. Only my beloved Beppo-Oma seemed to notice it, *she saw my soul*, and this is why I felt like I could breath and grow being around her. Today I know that as much as nature was just pure grace, light and joy, so was and am I. I feel that I am a deep mysterious part of it. And this is how my search for truth began: if I was a part of it, why did my heart feel so heavy, and why was I so sad? Why wasn't I just feeling light and joyful and graceful, like the flowers or Daddy did?

This question inspired me to start my journey of truth seeking, and today – about 25 years later – I have arrived at a point where I feel ready to write this book and share my journey of reconnection to this divine and loving life force, that I came to call God, with all of you beautiful souls who are truth seekers, too, and not comfortable with the way the world is running. I invite you to go back to your childhood years, when you were still discovering who you are and how you are connected to an infinite Source that made you get up no matter how often you fell.

Living my life, one day I came across a book from Wayne Dyer (and have after that read almost all of his books) who was quoting Rumi, and this is how I got introduced to Rumi's understanding of God or Source. Rumi's mystical understanding of God – I can honestly say – has brought me so much closer to Source, or the home in my heart. His Poetry beautifully describes who we are and how we relate to that infinite Source, God.

It is my deep desire that this book serves all of you beloved souls out there who feel or have felt the separation from Source as painfully as I did. I hope this book is an inspiration on your own unique journey back to who you truly are, back to yourself, your heart and how you are a divine expression of God with all your perfect imperfections here on Earth.

Throughout this book, I will use the words God and Source interchangeably, however, I always mean the same: This infinitely loving life force that created this universe, that created this planet and all it's creation, that created us, that *is us*.

Some thoughts and themes might seem overlapping. However, every word is carefully chosen to bring more awareness into our lives.

What is God?

So, let us start with the big question, which is what this book is all about: Who or what is God…? Personally, I am still on my way to explore about this amazing infinite vast divinity, but with everything I found out until now, my feeling of it is that God or Source is an infinite and never-ending well of divine unconditional Love, Light, Joy and Lightness, the fresh, healing, and releasing breath of the universe that nourishes all creation everywhere, including human kind, including me and you. As we start exploring further, let us first have a look at several dictionary definitions:

In most definitions I found when I did my research, God is defined as 'the One supreme Being', 'The Creator and Ruler of the universe', while other definitions include 'a being conceived as the perfect omnipotent, omniscient originator and ruler of the universe, the principle object of faith and worship in monotheistic religions'.

As we can see - and maybe this is not meant in a gender frame, but rather for easiness of explanation – it is referred to as masculine. This may not seem important at this point, however, somehow it emphasizes the importance and identification of humanity with gender.

I'd like to continue introducing my idea of God, so that we better understand what I am explaining in this book. I have already started giving ideas in my foreword when I talked about God as a divine order of unconditionally loving life force that breathes through all parts of creation. One thing I know for sure: God is far beyond from being one human being in male form, viciously punishing, torturing or even killing you if you do not follow the rules defined by human beings who call their words or actions 'in the name of God'. God was and is not creating wars between humans fighting against each other "in the name of God", no, this seems to be the confusion in humankind and their interpretation of what or who God is. In my opinion, it is simply a result of the separation from God.

Most Native tribes worldwide have a deeper and much more evolved understanding of God, as they see it in all creation, in nature. People who live in harmony with the Earth, like Native tribes or Nomads, seem to understand God/Source in a much deeper way, since they spend much more time closer to the Earth, walk barefoot, and live in harmony with the environment, the seasons, etc. I remember this beautiful Native American quote: "No tree would be so foolish as to create war between it's own branches." What a beautiful notion to see a tree as the entirety of humanity living as ONE and supporting and protecting each other…

What I know is that God does not prefer one race to another. Neither does it prefer one gender. The divine Feminine and the divine Masculine were both created to complete each other and are deeply interwoven, like the yin/yang sign shows beautifully. There is a reason that all was created the way it is, and I believe that the differences people see in other cultures, races, gender, etc. is a result of this wound of the separation from God, or a deep misunderstanding of what God is.

God is not something that will reward you for fulfilling conditions that were opposed upon you by other humans. Neither will it punish you for not fulfilling cultural norms. I rather experience God as an unconditionally loving Life Force that is constantly there guiding you, if you get still and choose to listen to this voice within your own heart. God loves you no matter what, it is rather humans who place conditions, and who created the concept of 'conditional' Love. As a result, humans somehow misinterpreted both words, God and Love.

I have come to realize that most monotheistic religions do not do justice to what God truly is, it only reflects their, sometimes limited, understanding of it, for we can only understand God in the way we understand ourselves. The more we connect to who we truly are, the more we will connect to God.

"I spoke to scholars and philosophers, but God was way beyond their understanding." Rumi

Sure, the founders did their best in trying to give their own understanding of what was given in divine messages, but they could only perceive it according to their own level of spiritual maturity and consciousness. And this conscious awareness was often controlled by cultural norms and power institutions, and reflected only how far the interpreters had come in understanding who they were and why they were here. God, the meaning of this sacred word, is far beyond of what the world has known and understood so far and maybe there are words to be yet invented to fully describe what it is. During all ages, there were amazingly evolved humans walking this planet, trying to convey the real meaning of God, including Jesus, Buddha, Lao Tzu, Gandhi, Mother Theresa, The Dalai Lama, the Elders of many Native tribes around the planet, John Lennon, and of course, Rumi. And these are only some, for there were many more. I came to believe that as humanity evolves spiritually, and becomes more conscious about who we are and why we are here, so will we find a new understanding for what God truly is, for God seems to be pure divine consciousness expanding alongside with all living creation including every single one of us.

When it comes to the world's great religions, I also truly believe that all religions or religious groups were and are trying their best in showing humanity the path to the light, but there is one important thing we need to consider: All religions, and even the teachings of the Saint, were defined and explained by humans, and what truly matters is the understanding and consciousness of those humans who wrote down these messages and – based on those explanations - wrote religion. The question is where they were on their own unique journey to reconnect to who they truly are as divine Beings, children of God, or how separated from God they felt, and were therefore – as a substitute – in need of (the illusion of) power. The reason I put this in brackets is that I believe there is only one true power, and this is our complete and whole union, our *oneness* with God/Source. This is where all true power, our power as divine Beings, stems from; all other definitions of power, such as status, money, positions and possessions, are in my opinion delusional perceptions of the Ego's understanding.

The term that kind of guided me in my understanding of this great creative loving energy is "the path towards the light", returning home. When I talk about Light, I talk about God or Source, meaning the divine goodness, the open heart, and the purity in every one and everything, this divine innocence you see in a baby's eyes that is pure Love and Joy. I am not talking about sexual innocence, meaning that you need to live in chastity or to be a virgin. In fact, Esther Hicks in her channelings of Abraham mentioned once that 'Jesus was no exception to the biological laws of human reproduction'. If that's true, then Mother Mary was not a virgin when she was pregnant with Jesus…

I feel that what was rather meant by Mary being a virgin is that she was good, pure, and innocent in her thoughts and actions towards all creation, a truly unconditionally loving and divine woman and mother that nurtured by her simple presence not only her child, but all life, all creation without judgment about who deserves it or not, and this was reflected in her radiant beauty. A beautiful feminine, loving and extremely powerful Being, with a strength we can only imagine, or only a mother would know that watched her child die. A loving-hearted and well-meaning woman who wanted the highest good for all, whether they were good to her or not. She transcended the physical duality, connected to the divine essence of which she was and is – God – expressing it through her grace, humbleness, unconditional love and service to others.

What if Mother Mary became so symbolic because she actually *IS* the representation of the divine feminine unconditionally loving sacred mother in general? She was and still is worshipped today, and what if she is actually showing that every woman who conceives a child, gives birth to it under extreme pain, and nurtures it selflessly until it can take care of itself, is sacred and to be worshipped? After all, this is the only way a man or woman can exist. Like Jesus, who is the Son of God and who valued both genders equally, for he spoke of everyone as children of God, is Mother Mary representing the sacred woman that is deeply connected to the Earth's intelligence, that contains the wisdom and the inner knowing through her intuition, and that radiates this Earth connected wisdom out through the peace and Love that she gracefully is? Is she actually a symbol for womanhood on Earth, conveying the greater meaning of the divine feminine that is yet to be understood by mankind?

Many Native American tribes were talking about how they admire and worship their wives, how they accepted and honored their women who are going through a lot of pain to bear a child. A Native American parable says 'A woman greatest task in Life is to connect men with source so that they feel the infinite. A mans greatest task on Earth is to protect woman so that she can walk the Earth unharmed.' They understand how much more connected women are to the wisdom of the Earth, a sacred Earth representing the loving life force of God, of all creation. And so to connect with Source as well, Native American men often initiate rituals for themselves in which they suffer much pain just so they can understand the mothers better, and also to get closer to that spiritual wisdom and knowledge that women have and that stems from our connection to Source. That does not necessarily mean that humanity has to suffer in order to be spiritually connected, no. We are spirit and all we need is to remember who we are, and there are many ways to get to this remembering. However, suffering is something that many awakened souls on this planet went through.

It is a woman's gift to feel deeply. So what if Mother Mary actually represented the Divinity of God suffering in all womanhood at that time, for women were – and still are in some cultures - considered less than men, which is an illusion creating separation and war within oneself who feels less or more than the other gender. And yet, if we look into the world today, what do we see? Are women loved, protected, and worshipped by men just because they are the ones giving Life? Are men doing their job in protecting women, so they can walk the Earth unharmed, for they are sacred mothers, knowing that without women, man could not be born? To understand God, and to transform the gender dis-equality we need to understand that God or

Source does not nourish one gender less than the other, for both are divine and equally valuable as part of divine creation, and are existent rather *within* us, no matter the physical gender of our body.

I truly believe that in truth we are inherently both, what the Chinese refer to as yin (the feminine) and yang (the masculine), we are pure consciousness combining the two within us. The judgment that one gender is better or stronger than the other, is a misunderstanding of God in humankind. Both, feminine and masculine are alive and were created. God created women to give life to both girls and boys, and for that and much more, women are sacred, and I believe therefore that Mother Mary is a metaphor for all womanhood, for all womanhood is sacred just like the masculine. The division between gender on Earth for me was a result of a misinterpretation of God, because the ego feeds on separation and is constantly trying to place itself 'above' another. Yet all is *One*. All is equally worthy and worthwhile. And by trying to divide or separate, we are separating from God, we only get deeper into the ego, the illusion of the physical duality here on Earth. To find closeness to God means to transcend all these old world beliefs and have the same respect for all.

I believe that God actually is the divine conscious essence in and of *all* creation, no matter what gender you are. It lives within the breath of life and as creation itself. In Chinese, Qi is equal to Life force energy, for it breathes through all that exists, every being, not only human, but all parts of creation, everything that lives in all dimensions, all realities. The little shy violet that blossoms in the shade of a rock, or the royal rose that is enchanting our eyes and hearts with her elegant beauty, both are an equally worthy expression of Source energy. The chirp of a songbird or the beautiful continuous sound of a Cicadae, both are divine creation worthy of Love. A little ant or a proud lion, God breathes through both the same Love. The flowing of a waterfall, the winds caressing the leaves of trees and making them dance in the sunlight, God is the spiraling breath of all creation. For God is all Life and represents Life everywhere. God is free will, and it is divine consciousness that we all are the creator of our own lives, whether we create deliberately or by default, by confusion or by understanding.

God is Love… and Love is all there is. I believe that the same that happened to the word of God, and how people have been conditioned to think of it, happened to the word of Love. In fact, in this human world, Love became a word that is conditional, and often it holds a connotation of pain and suffering, and is even reduced to romantic Love. We humans have been made believe that Love is not something we are, nor something that we deserve or is our birthright to experience. Love is often, at least in this human world, only given under conditions. Yet Love is so much more than that… Love is life, passion, happiness, flow, well-being, it is unconditional and loves the child who doesn't clean up her/his room just as much as the one that gets straight A's in class. It is a loving, creating life force, nourishing, nurturing and caring all without selecting or judging. It is inherently friendly and abundant, there is no limitation to it, other than those we carry in our minds.

God, or Source, is Love. It unconditionally gives it's gentle yet powerful force to anything in existence, not only 3-dimensional existence of what our eyes can see, but all cosmic existence, even the one beyond our imagination, beyond of what our eyes can see.

When a baby is born, no matter if in the animal realm, humans, flowers, trees, etc., whenever a baby is born, God breathes through this beautiful young Being with Love and passion, breathing life force through the mothers breath at the same time so she could nourish and care for the child, and breathing life force through the father so he can protect the mother and the child. Gods Love is deeply reflected in a loving family. There is a great saying from Khalil Gibran, the Lebanese poet:

"Your children are not your children. They are the daughters and sons of Life's longing for itself. They come through you but not from you. And though they are with you yet they belong not to you." Khalil Gibran

This shows in a beautiful way – other than the parental task of lovingly guiding the child but not 'owning' it - that God *is* every child, no matter which class it is born in, or which country or continent it was born on, and every child is worthy of Love. In a way, every child is bringing Source consciousness and energy to Earth, it is *Life longing for itself*. Every single child, I belief, is divine consciousness of Source coming to Earth and teaching humanity a new age. So in a way, our biological parents are our pathways to bring Source consciousness to Earth through their offspring, and the same goes for all parts of creation.

God is consciousness, and consciousness is everywhere. Like water or light it flows everywhere effortlessly. It is the conscious life force that tells a baby when it is time to leave it's mothers womb, it is the same conscious life force that opens a bud of a rose bush at the perfect time, that ripens the fruit on a tree in just the right timing, it just knows… It is all knowing, or omniscient. It sees, hears, feels and knows everything in existence; in other words, it is omnipresent, existing everywhere at the same time. For time, the linear time we know as human beings and by which our society is running – even though it seems real, is in some way a limited perception of all that exists. From a broader perspective, everything happens simultaneously in many different dimensions, since God is omnipresent and multidimensional.

Have you ever been out in Nature, just sitting underneath a tree or forest, or in a flower field, or next to an ocean or a flowing river or lake? What did you hear? If you are like me, you probably "heard", or rather *felt* this divine silence within you and surrounding you. The breath of the universe that is reflected in the waves of an ocean… The flow of life force… The smile of the colorful flowers in a wild flower field, or the birds singing in a wonderfully pine scented forest… isn't it all just beautiful? Did you feel free, calm and joyous there, did you feel nourished, loved, and friendly acknowledged? Did you feel the presence of God within you?

Did you ever feel judged when in Nature? If you answered this question with a no, you got it, for Flora and Fauna that is nourished by Source doesn't judge. Humankind seems to be the only species that does, however. But back to the nature scenes, what did you feel out there? Did you feel this loving force taking charge of your breath, your heart beat? Did you hear this divine silence when there is no man-made machinery or car noise or anything, just the breath of the gentle wind, bird songs, and natural sounds? How did you feel? Speaking for myself, these are the moments I feel inner peace in its most beautiful form.

Or let's say you are in your house, meditating. You quiet your mind, there is no more 'psychological noise'; you were able to switch off the mind chatter. And then you feel it, too. This beautiful, yet powerful silence, the stillness that feels so alive. You feel connected and ONE with all that is. The perceived separation in this 3 dimensional realm is no longer there, only oneness. And when you feel this deep connection with all creation, all that is, you no longer feel lonely. You are part of all, and all is part of you. This is when you are closest to what breathes through you. This is when you are can become one with that mystical energy that lives through us, within us, as us - God. Mystics often say that God is found in silence, and that the voice of God is not loud, or ruling or dominating, but rather soothing, gentle, and loving.

The reason I felt inspired to write this book is because ever since I heard Rumi's first poems, I deeply resonate with his infinite approaches to explain this mystical infinite source that is far beyond of what our minds could grasp or understand. And because it is so big, we can only feel it in little parts once we allow it in and claim ourselves to be part of it. We feel it once we allow ourselves to un-learn anything limiting that we have taken on from this world, when we reprogram all our old programming so to speak, and when we stand in our divine power as an infinite spiritual Being, accepting and acknowledging this infinite part of ourselves, our Source or who we truly are. We feel it in special moments all along. We feel it wherever there is Love. For wherever there is Love, there is God.

Again, everything I am sharing here is my personal understanding of the vastness of God, or Source.

At this point, for those who have not heard about him, I would like to introduce Rumi:

Rumi, or Jalal ad-Din Muhammad Rumi, was born 30 September 1207 and lived until 17 December 1273. He was also named *Mawlānā*, which means *Our Master*. Rumi came from the Mystical Islam, even though he did not call himself a Sufi, and still is one of the world's greatest poets who's poetry is the Light guiding me back into my divine (God)Self.

Rumi, known as a lover of humanity and a philosopher, said himself that he is not a Sufi, not Christian, not Jewish, not Muslim, for he might have already been aware that these 'categories' are only separating terms. It is also known that some of his passionate followers began a school of mysticism to encourage and celebrate his teachings—the Sufi branch known as the 'Whirling Dervishes'. Rumi apparently started to blossom with the coming of Shams of Tabriz, the love and spiritual mentor of Rumi's life. Before he met Shams, Rumi had been an eminent professor of religion and a highly attained mystic, while the presence of Shams in Rumi's life made him become an inspired poet and great lover of humanity. In fact, Rumi's poetry conveys a deep understanding of God, a definition of it so vast and infinite and loving I had never heard before.

So, why did I choose to explain my understanding of God based on Rumi's poetry, which hopefully also opens you up to a broader and vaster understanding of yourself? Well, when I started my quest for truth, Rumi was and still is the one whose words deeply resonate with my own feeling, my imagination of God. Rumi's poetry style is very romantic, gentle and sometimes provocative, loving, inspiring and door-opening, for it takes us back to our very beginnings, the cradle of creation so to speak, when there was and is the pure love of a divine intelligence creating, our Source, or God. We both are lovers of Life. We love our Source, and we see it in everything in Life. And through his mystical and beautiful words and my own sharing, my intention is to guide you, the reader and seeker, back home, back to your roots, back to God and your creator-Self, for this is who you truly are, have always been and always will be - a divine expression of God, a deeply loved extension of Source consciousness.

2

God and Confusion

As you know, all my Life – or as far as I remember - I have lived with a deep longing, a longing for connection with Love, with Truth… Not only once did I feel out of place in this noisy world, where things were – at least in my eyes – pretty out of alignment. I often felt like I was in a movie scene: people were running, chasing illusionary things, belonging to religions, yet judging others; there was no tree, no flower, no smile left for another. It was kind of a grayish dark, built up, busy, loud, and noisy world where people lived in closed boxes which they called houses, disconnected from Nature, from God, from themselves, from all that is. As a result of this disconnection, people felt lonely and separated, sad and depressed. These people looked like they were running and chasing, and yet they themselves longed for Silence, Truth, Kindness, Love, and Peace. There was so much suffering, so much doubt. This world was built up in a hierarchy where some were given more power than others, where titles and status was important to people, and even though the people with power had not the best interest of others in mind, they were chosen. A deeper understanding that we are all equally powerful was not known or promoted. Children grew up suppressed, and adults who wanted to express their desperate emotions about this world they lived in were misunderstood, called weak, ridiculed or even punished for being who they were. Parents were subtly made understood that their children hat to fit into the masses, be like everyone else, be obedient, don't be loud or different from others. Most of us grew up not being allowed who we truly are. It was a world of judgment and fear, loneliness and darkness… Many were and are afraid of truly and deeply connecting to others, for these others could leave us at one point, and this could be painful. Instead, many lived their lives feeling alone and unimportant. It was a world where emotions were not allowed to be shown or lived, and since everyone had emotions, we found ways to disconnect from them, and turned into functioning rather than truly living beings, also because self-expression was not encouraged. However, we humans are human because we feel, because we have emotions. If we don't allow ourselves to feel, we are not allowing ourselves to fully live, nor to be human. And God can apparently only be felt. So where was God in all this paradox of living?

Somehow I was waiting for this scene, this world to be over, so that there would finally be peace, joy, and alignment again, and the same harmony I saw when I was with nature. But this other peaceful world that included happy and life-celebrating people existed only in my dreams until then, and this dream was alive when I was out in nature alone far away from others.

I realized that there would always be disharmony in a disconnected world where feelings were not allowed, as long as this world existed within. So I would escape to my dream world as often as I could, and this dream world was completely different than the one I was confronted with here on Earth: This world of my dreams was green with blue sky and bright sunshine, and with happy, loving, joyous and lighthearted people that were kind to each other, caring, sharing and nurturing, living in thriving loving and connected communities. There was peace and beautiful harmonious gentle music in the air, the fresh air smelled like sparkling champagne, everyone felt welcome by smiles and scents of blooming flowers and vast greenery, the eyes indulged into green landscapes, abundant fruit trees and flowers, birds and butterflies, beautiful crystal round houses intermingling with nature, a deep blue ocean that flourished with wild life, whales and dolphins jumping out the clear waters, the breeze was gently caressing the leaves of majestic trees, everyone was deeply interconnected with one another. The temperatures were constantly pleasant, and people were wearing white long robes with golden ornaments, and everyone looked peaceful, happy and vibrating like pure diamond light. Things were moving slowly and in alignment with the peaceful flow of the universe. There were fewer people, but they were larger and their light orbs big and bright. They looked perfectly healthy and ageless, there bodies were moving gracefully and their eyes shone pure love onto everywhere they looked. It almost felt as if they were connected to each other telepathically, as if there wasn't even a need for language. They were kind and respectful towards every living creature they encountered: trees, butterflies, the ocean, the earth, other people, even those they had never seen before, women, men, children, animals, birds... The language they spoke, a soft loving melody, reflected the peace within their hearts, it sounded like Music, it was a perfectly orchestrated sound healing tone of kindness, peace, truth, and loving consciousness. This world was pure harmony. Everyone was welcome there, there were no strangers, only friends, and there was no fear, only love, compassion and understanding. Every tree was considered sacred and nature was allowed to grow in her divine intelligence without the interference of humans, there was no machinery, no cars, not anything that would disturb this peace... somehow the people were able to place themselves into different dimensions and realities by 'beaming' themselves to where they wanted to be... (a conscious intend, allowing their energy and physical body to be carried there)... Joyful and happy people living in Love and harmony with each other in a nurturing nature, such was the world I dreamed of...

This was my world, and somehow it kept me going for all those years while I felt that deep separation, the sadness of being misunderstood because of the way I felt, the loneliness of being in a dysfunctional world where everything that truly matters had yet to be discovered....

So I saw 2 worlds, one ruled by Fear, the other ruled by Love; one ruled by Ego, one ruled by the Heart. The first world seemed to me like people were separated from Source/God/Universe, the second one, where there was peace, people seemed like they were consciously living as divine incarnations of God. And I asked myself: Who or what is God and where can I find it? How and where can I find this beautiful, melodic, loving, graceful, green and pure world of my dreams? Did it exist somewhere else than in my dreams? And was it possible to bring God into the first scene of the world I experienced?

Then, one day, while listening to Wayne Dyer's wise words, he quoted Rumi and for the first time in this life, I was introduced to Rumi's understanding of God. The first emotion I experienced was Awe. Awe because it felt like my heart jumped out of pure bliss and deeply resonated with what I just heard. I even released tears because it felt so truthful – I was not alone in my quest for truth, for God. And then came gratefulness. Gratefulness that there were others, too, in their search for God and it's meaning. For the first time in my life, I felt understood by a soul who spoke the language of freedom, of Love, of God. Knowing I was no longer alone in my wild and vast idea of God, and of a peaceful world if we humans would only remember who we are, I started to research Rumi's inspirational work, and not only did it guide me along my search for truth, my self-transformation, but it set forth a whole new broader and vaster understanding of Life and God within myself, and of myself as a child of God.

Throughout my life experiences, and after reading several sacred scriptures, I came to understand God as the sacred, divine Source; Mother and Father at the same time, that we come from, are incarnated as, and go back to after our current incarnation, to a Source that is pure harmony. It is life given unconditionally, flowing through us as direct descendants from this Source as Love, light, beauty, vibrant health, peace, and alignment. So this Source is, equal to who we truly are, pure bliss, joy and infinite possibilities. And I asked myself; if we are all inherently it, this all-nourishing divine source, how come we are so disconnected from it? How come we have built a world where one is not allowed to show their authentic face of God, their unique beauty in the entire individual expression of Source that they are? Memories of my childhood arose and I kept asking: How come that I was hushed whenever I wanted to talk or express my feelings? Yes, I understood that my parents were overworked and had their own troubles, but how, if I wasn't allowed to express what I thought, felt and experienced, could I even be allowed to be who I truly am?

I felt that we in our entirety, all our emotions and feelings, everything is energy because it was changing all the time. Every thought is energy. I felt that we lived in a Quantum field of energy, and I saw it changing in the seasons of nature. I was also aware that energy could not disappear, nor could it be destroyed, it could only be transformed. So somehow I felt that this world and all the systems that had been created but no longer served humanity could be changed and transformed, and the big question was: How?

"Yesterday, I was clever, so I wanted to change the world. Today, I am wise, so I am changing myself." Rumi

Continuing this journey of Self-Discovery that we call life, I learned that it had to start within myself, that only I can *'be the change I like to see in this world'* (Gandhi), and so I started to embark on my own journey of self-discovery, of awareness, of cleansing and clearing all energy that did not feel good in my body and Being. This journey evidently set forth a deeper understanding of what happened on this planet and how the energy of these happenings is still stored in the collective consciousness. I also came to understand the importance of my own role on this Earth, and how – if I choose to live authentically and joyfully from my highest divine expression, being the Love that I always longed to see in this world – it could have a positive and uplifting influence on everything and everyone I meet, and on the bigger consciousness and the entire Quantum field.

So many wonderful incarnated and spiritual Angels helped me along the way, and I am forever grateful for their wise guidance. I started to understand how it was more about Being than doing, and that there was no such thing as 'trying to be', or 'working hard to get there', this is how our limited ego sees the things, and just by saying these words we create resistance. But our hearts... what was my heart here to tell me about who I AM, and what would it take to surrendering to its wisdom? Who was I in this world, and how did I fit in? What was God and how was I connected to it?

What I knew at that point was that God was so much more than a male human entity as it is defined as in many religions. To me, God is Love and breath, God is life and flow, God is goodness and grace, God is beauty and oneness, God is happiness and joy, God is compassion and kindness, God is surrender... And yes, intellectually I knew I am all of this, but I did not feel it fully integrated yet. I was aware that I am Love, I am Life, I breathe, I can put myself into flow, I am good and gracious... but how was I connected to God through it all?

"I tried to find God on the Christian cross. But he was not there.
I went to Muslim's Kaaba in Mecca. But God was not there either.
I went to the old Jewish synagogue, and the Hindu temple of idols

But I couldn't find a trace of God anywhere.
I questioned the scholars and the philosophers. But God was way beyond
their understanding.
I then looked deep into my heart. And it was there where he dwelled that
I saw him. God was nowhere else to be found."
Rumi

Thank you, Rumi! You are speaking out of my soul. Let's ponder about these wonderful lines for a little while… just feel into this passage. God is not something that our Ego's or our minds will ever understand; it is beyond that, for it can only be *felt*. In fact, somebody told me once: 'If somebody asks you who you are, and you can answer this question with a clear straight forward answer, then you haven't fully found yourself yet, you only understand this fraction of you. But you are way vaster than your current understanding of yourself, you are not your race, your color, your status, your titles… for words or languages can't do justice to how big, powerful, vast, worthy, and ever evolving you really are as a God-like Being'.

"When you know yourself, your 'I'ness vanishes and you know that you and God are one and the same." Arabi

This beautiful quote from Arabi, another one of the great Sufi poets, describes in a beautiful way that God's essence can not really be explained in words, for words have not yet been created to understand the infinite vastness of it. Arabi, Rumi and many others, including myself, looked everywhere for God – and I, for example, found glimpses of my divinity whenever I was in service of others. Once I helped a blind person to cross the street, and in the short but intense connection we made, I felt God. Another time I helped a blind person at an airport, and in our connection I felt the unconditional Love of God as well.

So, what does that mean to find God in our hearts? Is God rather a feeling then…? Or is it a state of inner peace within us once we understand and hear our whole range of human feelings and choose to be in charge of our own life in a blissful way? Is it the state of peace of mind that comes with understanding that we are infinite possibilities and here to explore and to expand our soul's consciousness beyond the existing structures of the world? And if that was the case, how do we get to this deep understanding?

I came to understand that in order to feel, we need to re-connected to our own feelings as well as those of others. The term to understand our and be connected to other peoples feelings is referred to as 'emotional intelligence' by Daniel Goleman, who devoted several books to this subject. We also call it empathetic or empathic. Usually those who understand and feel their own feelings on the deepest level feel and understand other people's feelings, too. Everything starts within us. We need to allow ourselves to feel the entire range of feelings, from powerlessness to Love, from despair to joy. Yet we have learned to avoid especially feelings that feel uncomfortable. We need to understand that feelings are simply energy, and whatever thought created the feeling, if we shift this thought, we can change the way we feel. We need to be in charge of our own feelings and no longer give external influences power over how we feel. So often we blame situations, the economy, election outcomes, other people etc. Yet we are the only ones in charge for how we feel. Let us explore this a bit further.

Wayne Dyer once mentioned this wise quote: *'If we change the way we look at things, the things we look at change.'* That means that we have power over how we want to feel by the thoughts we are thinking. Have you ever noticed that when you thought a positive thought about something or someone, you felt good, joyful, lighthearted and happy? There was no tightness or resistance in your emotions. Yet if you thought negative about someone or something, or you judged a situation, did you feel the tightness, or heaviness in your emotions, in your body? Have you ever tried that when you felt you were judging a situation or a person, and you realized that that wasn't beneficial neither to you nor to the other, and you shifted your thoughts about the situation/person into a more positive understanding, you actually felt better? Awareness about your thoughts can be learned by being attentive about how you feel in every moment.

Here is a beautiful exercise I heard once, told by Nora Herold, who channels the Pleiadians, a group of non incarnated star seeds and our loving family of Love and light: The process is called FOAL, like a young horse, and helps us to no longer resist feelings that feel uncomfortable, such as fear, guilt, shame and the like, for to be human means to *feel* emotions, only then can we truly feel God in our hearts.

The first letter F stands for FEEL. Every feeling, if we allow ourselves to fully feel and experience an emotion, embracing it lovingly at the same time, lasts no longer than 90 seconds. The reason why negative feelings persist is usually because we resist them for all kinds of reasons, and what we resist, persists. But when we allow ourselves to fully *feel* a feeling, it looses its uncomfortable grip or control over us. So now you feel that fear, and you realize you are ok nevertheless, that you still breathe, that you are in a safe space. It doesn't feel comfortable, but you are ok. And you keep breathing through it…

The second letter, O, stands for OBSERVE. Observe where you feel this feeling in your body, like you were pure awareness watching yourself from a bird perspective, and you scan your body where this feeling is. Again, while you do that, keep breathing through it lovingly, welcoming this feeling entirely as part of yourself…

Then, you ACCEPT it, that's what the third letter stands for, acceptance. Just accept yourself feeling this way, and accept the feeling/emotion without trying to explain or judging it or making it go away, just allow yourself to accept the feeling you are experiencing fully. And when we do this, LOVE flows in, the last letter of the process.

This exercise truly helped me in accepting feelings. Our star family, the Pleiadians, seem to be a great guide when it comes to remembering who we truly are by feeling ourselves again deeply, by stopping to operate from the mind, but from a much deeper feeling place of our Being.

When we get to a place where we can feel our own emotions and feelings with love, non-judgment, kindness, and acceptance again, we will automatically feel more expanded, safer, and in a way understood by ourselves and a bigger power. And if we continue this exercise with all feelings and emotions that are coming up, we will get kinder and more loving with ourselves every time, for we start to love our feelings as part of who we are. This will also open the door for more compassion in the world, because only when we understand and live through our own feelings, can we understand the feelings of others.

We are in no way victims of our feelings. Quite the contrary: We *choose* the way we want to feel by the way we *think*, for thought causes feelings to arise.

Eckhart Tolle said it this way: "The primary cause of unhappiness is not the situation itself, but our thoughts about it." It all starts with our thoughts, and the way we think is determined by our parents/caregivers, and the environment in which we grow up. Oftentimes, if our thoughts are not in alignment with who we truly are – Love and light – they are causing certain feelings and emotions within us, which, if not given awareness, can - in turn - cause physical ailments.

Buddha said: "You are what you think". Our thoughts have power; in fact, our thoughts have the power we give to them, because where focus goes, energy flows. So understand, if you think thoughts that are supporting you and all creation, thoughts that are kind and compassionate, you will feel balanced and peaceful. It is almost like you loose your density, your body lights up with the positivity and lightheartedness you are giving to Love. And when that happens, when God's Love can breathe freely through your illuminated light energy, you are usually living in a healthier body. However, if you give power to negative thoughts, be it conscious or unconscious, you will be 'advised' by your feelings, and later, if you ignore these feelings, by symptoms of your physical body telling you something is out of balance that needs your attention to be transcended and transformed into loving and supportive energy. A good question to help with this is: 'Are you controlling your thoughts, or are your thoughts controlling you?'

We are Beings of free will, meaning that we have a choice about what and how we want to think about no matter what, including religion. Did you ever try to think different over situations, people, happenings… or anything that gave you an uncomfortable feeling? And if you answer this question with yes, how did you feel your emotions shift? The resistance that suddenly faded away, the feeling of ease and acceptance that came with forgiving and felt like 'letting a person or situation off the hook'. And this in turn created a feeling of peace and freedom within you, a deeper understanding.

What if we could fully connect with God within us by being in complete peace with our feelings? When we embrace both, feelings that don't feel good and those that feel good, lovingly and accepting them as part of us without judgment, just experiencing their beauty and wisdom, we are allowing ourselves to stand more in our divine power, in other words, we are closer to God, to ourselves, and to all that is in this moment.

And so, to understand and find the path toward the light, to God, we need to understand first who we truly are in our thoughts, emotions, and in spirit. God said: I am that I am. So we choose what we want to be, and since we are energy, we can be anything we choose. We create by allow ourselves to *feel*, rather than being in our heads trying to explain. Once we understand who we truly are, a powerful, energetic Being of choice, and if we choose Love, I believe we will no longer feel the need to divide between 'race', 'religion', 'gender', etc. Because when we no longer feel separated from Source, we will no longer need to divide humankind into race or gender or any sort of difference. We no longer feel the need to divide between 'invasive' and 'native' people, or plants, or anything. When we see that all that is alive and nourished by an inherent life force, a divine order, including this beautiful planet we live upon, and when we allow ourselves to truly and deeply feel all that is, the divine creation of everything and everyone, we have found the Source that nourishes all of us, that lives within all of us and keeps all of us alive, no matter where we are from, or what you believe, or what your status is.

We all seem to have to go through a similar conditioning of separation here on Earth through established systems, like school, church, etc. So, if we don't learn how to feel from our parents, or in school, or other public institutions, how will we get there? I often have experienced people who are very emotional, and they, too, grew up in a world where it was unacceptable to feel, and where reason, or the mind, was the ruler. But then, what are we doing with these feelings inside of us if we can't share them or explain or even feel them? Many emotional Beings, as a result, choose to be numbing their feelings, or get into addictions, because the fear of going through uncomfortable feelings is just too great.

Speaking for myself, I was unable to truly connect to God through any religion, although Buddhism and the Tao Te Ching resonated with how I felt about it, although these scriptures are referred to more as philosophies since every one has free will and is not obliged to believe that way, while religion, as we have seen, tends to force it's beliefs onto others.

What if there was no intellectual understanding of God, and what if this is why philosophers and scholars weren't truly able to grasp what God in it's vastness really meant? What if God actually can only be felt in our hearts when we forget all we have learned about it? Elizabeth Gilbert said "God dwells within us, as us." And can we only connect with it if we allow ourselves to feel the full range of our emotions?

When we belong to a religion, we might believe that this religion will show us the way to God, without actually noticing that – at the same time by accepting the terms, rules and conditions of this religion - we might also limit ourselves. Plus, if others do not believe what we believe, we are prone to judge other religions as wrong, which can be seen by the many wars that have been fought in the name of God.

Is this why we have lost the connection to God, why humanity created wars between religions, because we have lost the connection to our feelings? And aren't feelings who we truly are? Aren't feelings the platform on which we connect to one another, no matter what our beliefs are? Is it possible that the need for religious wars can be ended once we are allowing ourselves to fully feel again and end the war against our own feelings? God is nowhere else to be found than in our hearts, and hearts do not think logically, they *feel*.

"Not Christian, or Jew, or Muslim.
Not Hindu, Buddhist, Sufi, or Zen.
Not any religion or cultural system.
I am not from the East or the West,
not out of the Ocean or up from the ground.
Not natural or ethereal, not composed of elements at all.
I do not exist. I am not an entity in this world, or the next.
Did not descend from Adam or Eve, or any origin story.
My place is the placeless.
A trace of the traceless.
Neither body or soul.
I belong to the beloved.
Have seen the two worlds as one.
And that one call to and know.
First, last, outer, inner.
Only that breath breathing human being." Rumi
That beautiful Oneness with the beloved that Rumi describes here seems to be similar to what other wise souls often referred to as pure bliss, and it is in emptiness with no thoughts and only our divine presence of Being where the feeling of connection to Source, this bliss, can be found.
"This Love is beyond the study of Theology.
That old trickery and hypocrisy
If you want to improve your mind that way
Sleep on." Rumi

These words – in my understanding - remind us that God is ever evolving and expanding with each breath we take, and in each loving gesture we give to others and us. Yet, if we continue to explain God from our limited Ego perspective, we won't be able to find it, we are 'sleeping on'.

Along my journey, there was an angelic guidance and presence that I came to know as God, and it always brought me back into my inner peace when I needed a break from this dysfunctional world I incarnated into. It breathes Love within my heart in each moment of life. It is the voice within my heart, the voice of my heart, and its guidance is noble and eloquent, accepting the mind as servant, while the heart is the master.

"I belong to no religion.
My religion is Love.
Every heart is my temple." Rumi

These sound like God's words. And imagine a world in which every single human Being would find Love, God, within their own hearts and realize that every heart is a temple… My hope is that this would be the end of religious wars and separation on Earth… When feeling and awakened human Beings see the sacredness and the divine beauty in every soul they meet again… What a beautiful world this will be!

3

God and You

"Do you know what you are?
You are the manuscript of a divine letter.
You are a mirror reflecting a noble face.
This universe is not outside of you.
Look inside yourself.
Everything that you want, you are already that." Rumi

The first time I heard these deep meaningful words, I felt such a deep resonance… Tears were running over my face, tears of being heard and seen and understood for who I am in my own infinity. I remember how much I felt like not being seen, heard or understood as a little child. I felt different than others, older than my years, younger than my fears, and somewhat outside of this world that I lived in. I looked for love everywhere, and most often found it in nature or with animals. I often observed rather than engaging in play. I often felt alone, and today I still hold myself in deep compassion of that little girl inside of me that felt so out of place.

I grew up in a family where feelings or emotions, let alone sharing and living them, was not encouraged. Whenever I wanted to share how I felt, I was called a 'trouble maker', even though my intention was only to share how something, a comment or behavior, made me feel, so that all involved would find a way to feel better. I felt that my feelings were ignored and misunderstood, and this made me feel alone and estranged from my own family or this world. And yet I had feelings that I couldn't ignore, even though I have tried. And there were feelings around everything. I felt when my mother was sad and overworked. I felt when my father as angry or rigid, etc. I felt all that and wanted to talk about it, when nobody else wanted.

The primary feeling in our home that I remember was tension and passive aggressiveness. This was a challenging environment to grow up in, since it frightened me and deepened my feelings of being alone and estranged even more. I did not feel safe. I one moment I really felt safe as a child was when we as a family, my parents and my sisters, were on our way to a little village festival, and everyone was looking forward to have a good and fun time. Once we parked the car and walked over to the playground, I saw my father taking my mothers hand, and they were walking like this for a while, looking at each other smiling. I remember the Love and bliss I felt in my heart in this moment, and almost as a result, I felt safe.

This is how I came to understand that what children probably need the most is a loving environment with parents or caregivers who love each other and show their love, kindness, and affection for each other and their children in a mutual exchange. And in this environment, everyone is allowed to express their feelings, for there are peace and harmony within and between all Beings. Out of my own experience, I believe that this is how a child will feel safe growing up.

Along my way of looking for the truth, I also became aware that our souls – before we incarnate back on this earth – choose our families and environments to grow up in, and I started to seek meaning in the way I grew up. I wondered what the lesson was that I had to learn going through this childhood. I came to understand, that maybe by feeling estranged and disconnected from the people and environment around me, I came to find the connection to myself, the divine inherent presence of God within me. And as I found it more and more within myself, I saw it more and more in everyone and everything else. This was my path to find the truth about who I am, and that God is not outside of me, but within me and within all creation.

"My cries of longing
My wails of sorrow
Are tormenting my soul." Rumi

I took these lines out of a longer verse, but they reflect how I felt. And knowing that nothing happens by accident, here is what I have taken away from my childhood feelings: whatever torments our souls, in other words, whatever gives us our most desperate or challenging feelings – therein lies our treasure. In my own case, this treasure was and is Oneness with Source, Oneness with ourselves, for we *are* God. When we feel one with Source or God, we will feel one with everyone and everything else. We will no longer come from a place of Ego, where we judge the insufficiencies or lacks of circumstances, whether it is parents or our environment, but we will come from a place of understanding. And understanding implies forgiveness toward all that seemed to make us feel bad, since we understand what the unfulfilled needs of those other people are, and that they could only give to us what they gave to themselves.

My childhood years in Kindergarden were rigid I remember, and I felt lonely and not seen as the one I am, even though I was in a group with other children. I remember being very skinny back then, and the woman in charge of our children's group made me eat more than I could handle. I remember her begging to stop to put food on my plate, knowing I couldn't eat that much, but she would ignore me. Maybe she meant well, possible remembering that she did not have enough food to eat, but it made me feel powerless. I kept telling her that I couldn't eat that much, but she didn't listen. One day, I still remember what the lunch was, she forced me again to eat up what she had given me, even though it was more than what I told her I could eat. I cried while eating, feeling that I was force fed, and while the other children had long finished and already gone to sleep, I was still sitting on the table as the only one, trying to finish my lunch. Then she came and put more food in my mouth, telling me unkind words about how she would punish me if I didn't finish, until my body couldn't' handle it any longer – and vomited it all out… I remember that despite my powerless and shocked feelings about being treated so inhumanely, I also felt a little bit triumphant at this point, for my body showed her that I was actually right when I told her I couldn't eat any more.

I know many of us grew up in a world where our feelings were not heard, nor appreciated or respected. We learned how to proof our point the hard way, and even then it might still not have been heard or seen but judged. Yet aren't children, and every human being, divine souls that need to be heard and respected in order to grow up healthy? How could we ever assume we would be helpful for somebody else as long as we believe we know better than this human being? This is where I believe emotional intelligence and compassion are essential virtues for a happier world.

Many of us probably had similar experiences about not being seen or heard or respected, and we all integrated these experiences differently. For many of us, the pain we felt and the defense mechanisms we've built around this pain, deviate us from our divine path here on Earth, and we might find ourselves later in life, feeling the same powerlessness or loneliness, only this time it was triggered by another experience, but it still points back to a childhood wound

The wound is the place where the light enters. Rumi

Feeling the divine truth within these words through my own experiences, it truly helped me to get to know myself, my own hurting feelings, and the treasures that grew out of them. We tend form our beliefs about who we are from how we have been treated by others, and what we perceived of who we are, which often creates a 'false identity' that we take on as a mask later in life. We think we are our false identity, and we learn to think, act and behave out of this false self of us, which is often also referred to as the Ego, instead of looking at ourselves from our heart. It makes sense that many of us loose our heart connection when we grow up in a way that we are not heard, seen, understood or our feelings not being respected. The pain and sadness we feel growing up in a seemingly cold and cruel world like is just too big, and sometimes if feels like we can't breathe in it… This has been my experience growing up in this incarnation.

Which brings me to another point: Breathing is the essence of life; the organ associated with breathing is the lung, the organ of 'life being fully lived'. I have often wondered if Asthma, which is so often seen in this world at this time, is actually a result of human beings feeling stifled in expressing who they truly are, in expressing their true feelings without fear of judgment? For when we are not allowed to express how we feel, our very life is somewhat stifled. Again, we don't really learn to do this, at least I did not. Many of us have equal experiences that when we do this as children, we are being ridiculed, belittled, misunderstood or even rejected from the group. I did not have many friends when I was little, and often I felt depressed and lonely. But something was there, and I found it when I went outside and experienced nature, breathing in the fragrant fresh air, connecting with flowers, birds and trees, and I couldn't help but feel lighter and happier in that moment. I saw the same behavior in dogs as a child, they seemed to be the happiest when they were outside, smelling everything that was around, being in the freedom and melody of trees, flowers and all creation, rather that inside a box.

Albert Einstein once said: "The most important choice we can make is to believe whether the universe is friendly or hostile." So for me, in order to heal and transform my childhood experiences, was and still is to know that I, that we all always have a choice – and that the Universe is indeed friendly when we choose to see it this way, starting within ourselves. I learned where people that I perceived as harsh are coming from. And what I found out is that it is often just the separation from who they truly are, the separation from their own feelings, from their hearts, that make them seem so harsh. So once we heal and embrace our pain, we will get to know compassion, and this will be the moment when we feel for ourselves and for others, for we are no longer separated.

I realized that I have a choice whether I want to continue to feel lonely and powerless, or whether I reclaim my power and uniqueness by re-connecting with my heart, by reconnecting with the God–essence within myself, within my heart, by embracing the Goodness of who I am with me accepting and honoring it first.

Rumi's words about us being a manuscript of a divine letter, and reflecting a noble face, encouraged me to look at myself with a deep gratefulness for all my experiences, no matter how beautiful or how hard they might have felt at the time they happened. I am all, and all these experiences make who I am, but they have no power over me. All my experiences create this beautiful divine Being, with God beating in my heart all along. My experiences shaped and polished me like a beautiful diamond. And this is true for all of us.

What if the words "the manuscript of a divine letter" actually mean the entirety of who you are, including all your good and painful experiences from this and past life times, and all your infinite potential of living in the full expression of who you could ever imagine yourself to be? When I studied the teachings of Buddha, I learned that our souls choose to consciously incarnate with a deliberate intention about this lifetime, in order for our consciousness to expand.

What if all our experiences, no matter how hard or painful they seem at the moment, are part of the divine letter, that deliberate intent of our souls, that expands our consciousness, so that we could find our way back home to our hearts, to unconditional love, to compassion, to joy, to oneness… and ultimately, to God? What if we even chose these experiences deliberately *in order* to find God?

What I can say is that through my own pain I came to remember who I truly am: A manuscript of a divine letter, a mirror reflecting a noble face, a valuable, worthy God-like expression of Source energy. And still today, I am integrating new experiences. I am still on my journey to expand out of my limitations, and as Abraham Hicks says, 'we will never get it done'. In other words, life, no matter if incarnated or in our natural spiritual energetic form, is a continuous journey of experiencing, integrating, learning, and expansion. If we choose to see it this way, if we choose to embrace our experiences as part of this divine growth, showing our noble faces to ourselves and everyone, while holding ourselves lovingly through processing pain or harsh times, we are on the divine path home to light, to God within us.

My advice for you, beloved reflection of God, is this: Dream, beloved Being, dream big, dream bold! Imagine you already *are* who you want to be. Embrace all that you are, all your experiences, feelings and emotions, with love and kindness. And trust that along the way you are seen, loved, and supported by your divine essence that birthed you in the first place – God. Continue to see beyond the veils of illusion and limitation, see your noble face, recognize God within you, and remember that you are the manuscript in all your experiences!

"Don't you know yet?
It is your light that lights the world." Rumi

4

God and Ego

"The Ego is always trying to hang on to what it knows, which is the past." Meg Benedicte

As mentioned in previous chapters, the ego is the false identity we have created based to the messages given to us in early childhood years. It is the false self, the mask we put on in this world, in order to fit into our family, school, and the larger society. The ego is a mental creation therefore, and all it knows is past experiences and future worries, but it doesn't understand the power of the present moment. It does not see the truth of who we are as divine infinite Beings. To understand the ego better, here are some explanations of what it is defined as.

"Your ego is your conscious mind, the part of your identity that you consider your "self". If you say someone has a big ego, then you are saying he is too full of himself. The ego is often being confused with 'megalomania' and 'vanity' and all kinds of other nasty things. But strictly speaking it is a psychological term popularized by Sigmund Freud meaning the conscious (as opposed to the unconscious) mind, or the awareness of one's own identity and existence. The ego is also referred to as an inflated feeling of pride in your superiority to others." ('Vocabulary.com')

When we talk about conscious mind, would you agree that most of us have a very limited belief of who we are, in other words, would you say that your awareness about our own identity and existence is fairly limited based on the messages we received when we were little? As I said before, if we can answer the question 'who are you' based on our titles, religion, race or any other word promoting separation, we are probably answering from our limited understanding of who we truly are.

Let me consider another definition from Dr. Wayne Dyer that brings us closer.

"No one has ever seen the face of ego. ... The ego is only an illusion, but a very influential one. Letting the ego-illusion become your identity can prevent you from knowing your true self. Ego, the false idea of believing that you are what you have or what you do, is a backwards way of assessing and living life."

According to Dr. Dyer's words, the ego is an illusion. An illusion therefore, because this false self is created by our very early experiences in life, and often far deviated from who we truly are, depending on how unhappy or traumatizing our childhood experiences were and how we handled them, and how the environment in which we grew up influenced us. The ego is an illusion that separates us from our true self. Not only because the ego only knows our past experiences and – based on those - tries to protect our survival in taking limited decisions for the future, but also because the ego tends to rationalize. And yet, most of us have learned to be in this mental space of our false self, to create and live our lives from this space, to reason and rationalize rather than to trust our feelings and be guided by them. When we are acting out of ego, we are acting out of limitation, and fear, and for many of us, this is also what was being role-modeled to us by our parents and our society. So the ego, to many, is perceived as the real Self, the Self that can be trusted, while it is very limited in understanding who we actually are.

Did you ever asked yourself why the poor remain poor, while the rich get richer? This is a perfect example to show how the ego works: If you were poor when you were little, and money conversations were unpleasant because there might have not been enough, your ego will remember that lack is the truth, and it will create life out of the thoughts you learned about lack. However, if money was abundantly there when you were little, and you ego grow up knowing 'I can have whatever I want', this is the energy from which you will live your life later in your adulthood.

"Reason is powerless in the expression of Love.
Love alone is capable of revealing the truth of Love and being a lover.
If you want to live, die in Love.
Die in Love, if you want to remain alive." Rumi

I pondered a long time over these important words. What I came to feel when reading these lines is the word surrender, to surrender the ego. Wayne Dyer said it so beautifully: E G O in other words means Edge God Out. So when we embrace and then lovingly detach from our ego, our false self (die in Love), we surrender to something way bigger (but that the ego can't grasp with it's limited understanding) than can emerge from there. We surrender to our God essence within. To transcend the ego, to die in Love, meaning we surrender to Love/God, which is our true essence felt in our hearts, we remain alive.

"Your task is not to seek for love
but merely to seek and find all the barriers within yourself
that you have built against it." Rumi

As shown, we all grow up in a way that created a false self, a being that reflects the limitations of the messages and feedbacks when we were very young. Scientist say when we are baby's, our brains are in Theta wave state, which makes us like a sponge, absorbing and integrating messages from our environment, micro to macro. Even in our mothers whom we will absorb voices, emotions, and feelings of our mothers. If the primary emotion of a mother is fear, the baby will be naturally fearful. One can also see this as energy. Nothing is separated from each other, everything is interconnected. So, if the baby grows up in a womb and/or environment of fear, it will naturally feel these emotions, too. Babies pick up on the energy of the environment, and so do little toddlers, which is often reflected in their well-being. Up until the age of 4, the child is in a space where it is very connected to Source, pure and innocent, and as I mentioned before, if the environment of a child is unconditionally loving, supportive, affectionate, caring, and joyful, the child will create healthy thoughts about life and the world. However, if the child is born in an environment fear, anger, aggression, and powerlessness, it will as a result be fearful as well, for it perceives this primary emotion as the truth. Out of such an environment come thoughts of 'I can't trust', 'I am not safe', 'the universe is not a friendly place' etc. Whatever the parents feel or live as their primary thoughts, the child will pick up on it and continue to live it later in life, if it doesn't become aware that all of it is 'only a programming', and that the brain can be re-programmed at any time if we start looking deeper.

"The Ego is a veil between Humans and God." Rumi

One of my favorite learned wisdom pearls is this: "In our first half of life, we are defending our ego/False Self, and in the second half of life, we begin to remember our purpose and start living it."

The ego is a false shadow personality (Meg Benedicte), it only exists in past and future, it is an illusionary self that is constantly trying to keep us within 'our comfort zone', within what we, or the ego, knows; and what the ego knows is the sum of all it has experienced, and the thoughts and defenses it built around these experiences.

Here is a beautiful quote coming from Lao Tzu: *"When you feeling depressed, you are in the past. When you are feeling anxious, you are in the future. When you are in the present moment, you are in peace"*.

The ego only knows past and the fear of the future based on our past. Yet, when we come back into this moment, into the here and now, we are in peace. And in this peace, all creation is possible. Because when we look around us, unless we are in regions on this planet where humans are in war with each other, there is nothing to fear. We realize we have a roof over our heads, we have enough to eat today, we have clean water to drink, we have – if we are lucky – maybe our loved tribe around us... and we will realize that we've had everything all along. And when we consciously choose to be in the present moment, we can choose a different basic belief, such as 'the universe is friendly', if we feel it is not. Every moment is a new beginning.

So when we choose to live in the here and now, when we are truly present in this moment, we are powerful and creative. We come home to us. Of course, the ego will try to drags us back to either the past or the anxiety of the future, but we can choose to be in the here and now by becoming aware of the present moment. Breath is a powerful tool to remain in the present moment.

Let's take a closer look at this world or society we live in here on this beautiful planet Earth: How do you feel? Do you feel it was created out of our hearts where there is the power of unconditional love and support, or do you feel it has been created out of ego, out of limitation and lack?

When we look at the school system: What do we learn? Do we learn mostly about physics (what the eyes can see, but what is by far not all that exists), rules and limitations, competition and lack? Or do we learn about metaphysics? Do we learn about Love, Happiness, Sharing, Community, Co-operation, Forgiveness, Moon Cycles, the natural Flora and Fauna of the Earth and how we can nourish every one with her abundant goodness, or how to live our full potential or even be ageless? Do we learn connection or separation? Do children learn to be happy? Do they learn the truth that they are powerful creators? Or do they learn that they have to work hard, that they have to compete in order to get a decently paid job?

I believe most of us would agree that the systems in this world, including school, health care, governments, religions, economics, politics and so on were made out of the ego, a rational and therefore limited understanding, and even though the founders – many years ago – sure did the best they could according to their understanding of the world, those systems reflect a very limited understanding of who we truly are.

I believe that the same way mankind has created these crumbling systems out of the ego, we are here to create new systems, now corporations that are in service of humanity, rather than exploiting it. So that where there was competition, there will be sharing, where there was hatred, there will be love, where there was ego, there will be heart, where there was lack, there will be abundance, where there was loneliness, there will be happiness and connection.

And it all starts with us, and of becoming aware of the creative power of the present moment. Imagine everyone would get her or his share. Imagine even religions may turn back to the original idea of their founding: To bring humans back to the light and love that they truly are, considering every being as precious. If we can bring ourselves more and more back into the present moment, into our hearts, I believe we have a chance to live from a space where God no longer exists as something outside of us, but within us, as us.

I remember a beautiful story I heard from an African tribe. The teacher is telling the children that they are going to do a competition. The one that runs the fastest to the fruit basket on the other side will get it. The children took each other by their hand and started walking towards the fruit basket together. The teacher asked: 'Why are you doing that? Doesn't one of you want to win the basket?' The children replied: 'How could we enjoy the fruits if only one of us can eat them and be happy, and the other ones will remain hungry?'

Who, would you say, is the teacher here? And doesn't this teaching contain a much broader wisdom – that maybe it is time we allow our children to be our teachers, while they can rely on their parents as the ones protecting them and loving them unconditionally, rather than projecting own limitations and fears onto the child?

5

God and the Idea of Heaven and Hell

As long as I can remember, I pondered about the truth of the belief that after death, we are either going to heaven or to hell. Soon along my journey of seeking the truth, I got to know physical places here on Earth that – to me – kind of reflected heaven and hell. When I was in a green, beautiful, and untamed environment where wild flowers bloomed, where birds where singing, where nature was allowed to breath and exist, where there was only the natural sound of wilderness, I felt happy, I felt 'in heaven'. The same would be true to me if I stood in the quiet night under millions of stars shining, hearing only the symphony of 'cosmic music' and maybe some night birds… or when I stood on a natural beach where I only hear the breath of the ocean, the seabirds, shells and other ocean treasures around me, surrounded by dunes and maybe forest further back from the water… I feel peaceful there, in heaven. The same peace I hear in classical music, or in a forest where birds are singing, the wind would move the trees gently, as if it was dancing with them, while the trees, at the same time as they are dancing, sounded like they whispered a gentle truth, the truth of existence, of life, of love, of God… Wherever there was no human made disturbance seen, felt, smelled, or heard, I was home.

The opposite was true for me walking along polluted, busy streets in a noisy city where you hear jackhammers and aggressive manmade machinery, hectic people with unhappy facial expressions, etc. Also when I hear aggressive music, I feel how this disrupts the energy within me and everything, for everything is energy and responds to energy… This, to me, feels like hell.

Here is how both environments make me feel: In the first one, my heaven, I feel connected, safe, lovingly held, home by hearing the gentle truth of my intuition, or my inner voice. In the second, what I would call hell, I felt heavy, unsafe, I could not feel or think clearly, I could not breathe easily, I just felt the need to get out of there as soon as I can…

And from there, I started thinking about what if we actually created heaven or hell on Earth from our minds? Clearly, the peace and silence of untamed nature allowed me to feel peaceful and in alignment, to enjoy the present moment with all it's beauty, and to breathe and create. The disrupted places, however, made me think and feel differently: was it the disconnection of humanity from nature that actually created an unhealthy, polluted, noisy environment, in which we can't think clearly or feel peaceful? Was it busy minds – busy with fear and 'noise' that created these noisy cities and places as a reflection of them? And was the 'noise' of these minds coming from ego, from all the fears and limitations that existed in it?

In pondering about my questions, I learned along the way that there are two main emotions from which everything, every other emotion or feeling, stems: Love or Fear. When we are in a heart space and mental state of Love, of joy, of kindness and peace, we feel, as a result, oneness, connection, compassion, joy and unity. In other words, we are in heaven, for we feel peaceful, alive, happy, aligned, powerful, trusting and creative. We feel in love with ourselves, with the environment surrounding us, the food we eat. We feel in love with the world, which is reflected in everything we feel, are, see, speak and do. We believe the universe is friendly and kind, and we feel safe and supported by life itself. This is heaven...

When we are in the energy of fear, however, from which lack, scarcity, competition, judgment, frustration, anger, disconnection, separation, etc. derive, we are in a mental state of hell, for we feel disconnected, worried, anxious, fearful, powerless, doubtful, etc. Our thoughts create our feelings, our feelings create our vibrational frequency, and – since life is a mirror to our vibration, we will attract more of what makes us feel 'in hell'...

As I looked at both concepts from this perspective, I do not believe that heaven and hell are places we go to. They are in fact mental spaces that create states of Being, a vibrational reflection of the thoughts in our minds.

I would even say that when we are aligned with our divine Source within, with God, knowing we *are* God, we would feel like we are in heaven on Earth, because we will look at the world with different eyes. We will see, observe and integrate what is going on with love and compassion, but we won't feel disempowered by it, neither will we feel the need to judge, compare, or measure. We would observe everything in the eyes of love and therefore with awe, and we might even find a higher meaning in all that happens. We are anchored in the divine love of our hearts, where there is trust, faith, understanding, meaning, and compassion.

However, when we are disconnected from Source, when we are in a mental space of hell, then – I believe – we would feel that the world is hostile, that there is no one understanding or helping us, that we have to carry the whole burden of life and this world alone, in short, we feel powerless and victims of life. As a reflection, our vibrational frequency, our energy will feel heavy, dense, powerless, etc., and the experiences in our lives, which are always a reflection of our vibrational frequency, will just bring us deeper into the believes we have.

So, heaven is our mental state once we made our heart the master and our mind the servant. It is the space where we are in the present moment, consciously choosing our thoughts, and where we become the creator of our experiences. The heart, once it is free of pain and other energetic blockages (which is possible by doing the FOAL process explained earlier in this book), is our direct connection to Source. When we vibrate in the energy of unconditional Love, compassion, understanding, and joy, we are in a state of heaven. Our thoughts are positive and supporting our connection to all that is, our emotions feel balanced, joyful and blissful. There is no need for any distraction, like TV, alcohol, tobacco, drugs, etc., we have become our own best friend, our own divine parents, our own source of happiness, and as such, we are self-sustained, and we enjoy being in our own company.

"Between my Love and my Heart
Things were happening which
Slowly, slowly
Made me recall everything
You amuse me with your touch
Although I can't see your hands,
You have kissed me with tenderness
Although I haven't seen your lips
You are hidden from me.
But it is you who keeps me alive
Perhaps the time will come
When you will tire of kisses
I shall be happy even for insults from you
I only ask that you keep some attention on me." Rumi

While the first 3 phases are in some way explaining our connection to our heart – to God – the last phrase could be understood as the mind trying to make sense out of this vast, beautiful unconditional Love available to each and every one of us, and a certain fear that it will disappear, since the mind operates out of what it knows; and in most cases, what it knows is lack. Yet God's Love for us is unlimited and unconditional, it just exists and keeps growing with each breath we take, and each tiny act of Love we share, be it with us or with others. *"Yet it is you who keeps me alive"* is a beautiful statement of our divine self, God within us, a part of source always connected to it, that is there existent no matter if incarnated or not. It just is. All we need to do is remember this part in us, start to trust it again, and let ourselves be guided by it.

The opposite of heaven - hell - is what most of humans – including myself – have – as a mental state - been living on this planet for a long time. It is the stage in which the heart is the servant, and the mind in fear is the master. But what good master can the mind be to us if it doesn't even understand or grasp who we truly are, if it only knows what it has experienced? And if we have never experienced God/Source in our hearts, if we never felt the alignment with this creator energy that loves and nourishes all of us unconditionally, how will we get to reconnect to God from a mental place?

When we make our mind our master, which is what we have been conditioned to do, we are in other words giving more value to our ego, to all our lived experiences, judgments, and limitations, rather than to limitless possibilities. It is today a scientific fact that the mind can't grasp who we truly are, and it is often having a very limited perspective of all possible things. Plus, the mind is primarily coming out of fear and limitation, rather comfortable remaining within the boundaries of what it knows, for this feels safe. Yet when we make it the master, what good do you think can come from there? What good do you see in this world?

So, what we need to understand is that when we make our heart the master, or in other words, we reconnect to God by feeling our heart frequency, the frequency of pure Love, and by choosing to live from this space in every moment, we can then become aware of our true essence of a limitless divine creator, a being of Love and Light. We will remember our pure essence of divinity, the vastness and divine power that we truly are. We will no longer feel fear, but trust, faith, support and oneness. We will feel compassion, joy, and happiness where there was once pain, loneliness, and doubt.

This could change everything, including the way the world is running. Coming from the heart as the master, we would then use our mind – our mental intelligence - to create from our loving heart. And as the heart knows only Love, what we will create will serve everyone, for it is created from pure Love and joy for all creation. Would this be the moment that cities become greener and less noisy again, where people connect and create loving and supportive communities, like it is already the case in many places? Would this be the time humans stop cutting forests, realizing these are the lungs of our Earth? Would this be the time humans would stop to trim trees knowing every tree is a highly intelligent and conscious Being that knows perfectly how to grow? Would this be the moment that nature's divine intelligence will be recognized again, and respected, and that more sustainable resources would be used and mankind would stop exploiting the Earth, our sacred mother?

What would it need to create a world of peace and community with kind awakened people? In this context, let us take a quick look at the word 'intelligence'. Up until now, a lot of value was placed on the so-called IQ, the intellectual, mental, or cognitive capacity of humans. I remember that in college, those with a high IQ were the most celebrated. But if this is such an important virtue, why are those with a high IQ not truly happy? They might have created a lot of things or technologies, but why would many of them not live happy lives?

Because the IQ differs from the EQ.

I am a firm believer that what is way more important to find connection and alignment again is a high EQ, emotional intelligence. Emotional intelligence means to understand your own and other people's feelings, and to handle them in a compassionate way, so that everyone feels understood and respected. I believe that we will get much further with a highly evolved emotional intelligence, for after all, we humans are not machines or robots. We are human because we *feel*. So when our EQ is high and our feelings are aligned with understanding, compassion, love, and kindness towards one another, we will be able to truly understand each other and the underlying emotion of everything, we will be able to truly connect again.

Some of the most amazing teachers on this planet, Louse L. Hay, Dr. Wayne Dyer, Matt Kahn, just to name a few, all had and have a very high EQs, and their work reflected the love they had and have for humanity, for they are in service to others. I believe when our EQ is high, not only will it benefit a reconnecting humanity, but it will bring forth the remembrance of how important service to others is. I had the joy to work with so many amazing empathic clients over the years, and all of them had one thing in common: A high EQ and the need to serve humanity in a bigger way, which implies that we become the divine version of ourselves.

Compassion, as explained, is a big component of emotional intelligence, meaning that one understands and embraces his own and the feeling of other people in a respectful and safe way. Compassion can therefore only be thriving once we humans allow ourselves to feel the entire range of our feelings and emotions again, and to be able to handle them with love and kindness not as something threatening, but as an important part of ourselves that deserves Love. All feelings and emotions (e-motion, in other words, energetic flow) are energy. So if we allow ourselves to fully be with the energy of whatever we feel, no matter whether it belongs to fear or Love, we will – at the same time – strengthen our EQs. I would even say, at least this was my personal journey, that if we allow ourselves to fully be with all the emotions that come out of fear and therefore don't feel good, and embrace them, lovingly holding and breathing through them, allowing them to dissipate in the process, we will be able to experience the higher vibrating emotions like love, joy, happiness, connections, compassion etc., even more, because we have transcended the energy of the lower, heavier vibrating feelings, and therefore made room for what feels good.

"Our biggest quest is not to seek love, but rather all the barriers that we have built against it." Rumi

When we allow ourselves to feel the lower density emotions, rather than repressing them, when we are truly able to embrace them with love, not only will we find compassion, but we will 'find God', in other words, we will connect more with our divine essence within, through compassion and the permission to feel with the intend to see and transform all into Love.

We are humans. What make us human are our feelings. If you deny feeling your emotions/feelings, you reject your humanness. If you embrace your feelings and allow yourself to feel the whole wide range from joy to despair, from love to fear, from power to powerlessness, you will realign with the truth of who you are – and who you are is Love. As you do this with yourself, you will also be able to understand the feelings of others, show compassion and help, which in turn will create connection.

As long as you deny your feelings, or even just certain ones that feel too painful for you to feel, you will continue to allow them control over you, and you won't be able to transcend the energy of it. In other words, you keep the barriers you have built against love intact, which will in turn create more separation. So, to fully understand and be able to handle your own and other people's feelings from a space of divine Love and acceptance, knowing how they feel because you have allowed yourself to feel it, will help you to feel more connected to others, as well as your heart, or God. It is proven that people with a high EQ are happier and healthier individuals than those with a high IQ. To have a high IQ, we don't necessarily need to come from a heart place, although coming from a heart space – I believe - might even increase the IQ more, because we are more loving with ourselves. But to have a high EQ, we need to know and accept ourselves as feeling Beings, and we need to approve of our feelings and embrace them. I believe that, in order to develop a high EQ, we need to allow ourselves to feel and come from a place of more connectedness with others and ourselves. And if we continue to do so, we will get closer to who we truly are – Love – with each time we are accepting feelings and allow ourselves to deeply feel it. I truly believe that this is the path to peace on Earth… we are transcending the limited perceptions of the ego and get back into the fullness of what life has to offer.

Some may ask, but what if these emotions feel very painful? What if my fears or other emotions that feel terrible, like despair, powerlessness and the one, are so big that I think I will die when I feel them again?

First of all, remember Rumi's words about *dying to remain alive*. Yes, if you allow yourself to fully feel again, creating a safe space around you while you do this sacred healing with yourself, you might feel like you are dying, but your fears will die with you, for they will loose control over you by no longer denying them. Start the FOAL process described earlier in the book with little things that don't feel frightening to you, and see how you feel afterwards. When I do this, I always felt lighter and more peaceful, and with an inner sense of freedom.

Also, remember that suffering is a choice. You do not have to suffer in order to attain wisdom or inner knowing. So choose wisely, speak to yourself as if you were your divine parent, telling you everything you wished you would have heard when you were little. Choose empowering words for yourself. And know that when I say 'suffering' is a choice, it is deeply connected to not allowing yourself to feel. Many of us think 'we will suffer when we feel', and therefore, it is safer to be in an ego space, where everything is rational. But I have seen people dealing with huge inner anger, aggression, etc., and denying themselves to fully feel them, yet having choleric outbreaks every time they were triggered. As long as we do not embrace and welcome these feelings and allow ourselves to fully feel them, they will continue to have control over us, and every time there is an external trigger, they will come to the surface again, and you will suffer. And maybe you will make others suffer, too, because most often people that are hurting themselves are prone to hurt others. Go into your heart, beloved One, remember you are love, have compassion with yourself and that inner child that feels powerless, and hold it with love and acceptance until it dissipates, knowing that you are safe and loved now.

And as a last notion, remember that fear can be translated into
F = false
E = evidence
A = appearing
R = real.

Until now, would you say that most people – including myself – have been slaves of our own fears? What if fear is just a big illusion that we have the power to transform just by allowing ourselves to feel?

Now, stop for a moment and look at this world. Where have humans placed more value on, would you say it is the IQ, the intellectual/cognitive intelligence, or is it emotional intelligence? If you answered that it is the IQ, is it any wonder that the world is in so much chaos? Is it any wonder that you feel misunderstood by your own psychologist, because they don't need to do an EQ exam before trying to understand others? Is it any wonder then, that children are forced to do all the same in school systems, whether they are sportive and like sports, or they are more artistic, like I was? What message does this send to humans, especially highly sensitive and still forming children? In my case, the message I received was 'you are not allowed to be who you are. Your special gifts have no value, or they are not good enough.'

Think about the Medical system. One of the most severe byproducts of a diagnosis is fear. Now, do doctors understand the fear of their patients? Do they work with their patients to dissolve their fears, or do they instill more? Do doctors have to absolve an exam in emotional intelligence, so that they could truly understand their patients? Isn't it of utmost importance for a sick person to feel understood in their fears, to not feel alone, and to have someone on their side that helps them transcend the fear into trust, that all will be well again, once they shift what is out of alignment in their mental/emotional body that caused the dis-ease? There are so many amazing studies out there today, just go into the evidence coming from for example Dr. Joe Dispenza or Dr. Bruce Lipton. The scientific facts they brought to the surface left me in awe…

When you look at this world, what would you say? Do most people live in a space of heaven, or hell? Do we live mostly in a space of fear, or love? What do you feel needs to shift to create a world of love and heaven on earth?

Here is a story that I heard a long time ago that perfectly illustrates the idea of heaven and hell and helped me to get to a deeper understanding. It is the story of a priest and a prostitute: They live in the same apartment complex, opposite of each other, and they can kind of see each other through each other's window. So every morning the Prostitute gets up and prepares to do her work, and she sees the Priest through her window preparing for his day, and she is filled with a sense of awe and love and sacredness, she feels grateful for the work he is doing. And every morning, the priest gets up and sees the prostitute. And he is filled with judgment, and belittlement of 'if this poor lost soul could only find God', so his thoughts are of separation, lack, and limitation, all of what he believes she is lacking and missing. Then, one day they die, and she goes to heaven, and he goes to hell. And when he gets the chance to talk to St. Peter, he asks: What is happening here? I was dedicated to God and the truth and I did my sacred work in this world every day, and I go to hell and she went to heaven, while she was a prostitute doing all this sin? And St. Peter replied: Every morning, you got up and all you saw, what you were filled with was judgment, sin, lack and separation, so that's what you were activating, that's what you were already living, you were already in hell, and so you just manifested it. She, however, she got up all she saw was Love, truth, sacredness and gratefulness, and so she did the work she did, but she was filled with gratitude and love and light, so she was already in a space of heaven while on Earth and so that's what she has manifested.

Thoughts have power.

Pause for a moment and imagine a world of peace. How do people behave? Are they loving, kind, and compassionate with themselves and others? Do they feel and understand the feelings of others? This journey could be so joyful and beautiful. Imagine children would be encouraged to feel the way they do again, none of their emotions would be repressed or criticized, they would be allowed to be who they are in the entirety of their feelings, knowing that feelings are energy in motion, they come and go, but if they don't get repressed, they won't create energetic blockages in our energy… Every single one of us could return towards joy, which is our natural state of Being, just like Love. And joy and Love are not feelings we go to, they are who we are…

6

God and Newborn Life

Yesterday I went to a flower shop – I felt kind of blue in the morning and flowers always help me to strengthen my connection to who I truly am, to my divine essence – and I saw a baby stroller at the entrance that a mother quickly left there while she was looking for flowers. In the stroller was her little baby, a beautiful pure and innocent baby-boy of Love and Light. I looked into his big blue eyes and when our eyes connected, I couldn't help but feel this overwhelm of unconditional Love for this beautiful pure loving bundle of Life force. Oh what a joy. This bright Being just came from Source… The purity, the innocence, the curiosity, yet a deep knowing of his belonging and the resulting joy brought tears to my eyes… What an amazing teacher this baby was to me…

It reminded me of who we truly are before we got conditioned by society and all the limitations we might take on from caregivers or school, allowing layer after layer of dark limited energy cover up our inner light and pure beauty… So for me, while I was with this beautiful pure joy of life, the ever present question arose again: How can I connect back to this divine essence, this bright joy, this illuminating knowing, this divine purity, this beauty, this fulfilling feeling of belonging…?

The only answer I got was 'letting go of what I am not'… Again, Rumi's quote *'releasing the barriers we have built against love'*…

Every newborn baby is pure Love, and all it wants is to be loved. God does not divide children into poor or rich, into black or white, red or yellow, girl or boy, every child is an extension and expression of pure Source energy. All that a child needs in order to grow into a psychologically and physically healthy human Being is unconditional love and affection. In this pure and blissful innocence, they absorb everything that is going on in their environment, including energy, sound, tone, frequency, and the like.

The challenge is that most babies are being born into a world where the main emotion of fear – and all other emotions stemming from it like anger, despair, powerlessness, aggression, frustration, depression lack, jealousy, etc., is still prevailing.

There is another challenge for little babies I observed over the years. I know that all parents are doing the best they are able to. But does it need more consciousness to raise a healthy human being into this world? Think about it: For almost everything on this planet we need a license. But how many parents, before they have children, have actually truly learned to love themselves, to be in peace with themselves and the world? How many have learned to look after their needs as much as they look after others?

I've had the pleasure to meet so many wonderful parents along my way, parents to whom it was a conscious decision to dedicate their time to raise a child while loving themselves and each other, and I know that there are more and more children being born into families that are conscious about the childs needs and have the capacity to fulfill them, because they are aware of their own needs, and how to take care of them. Many parents I got to know were taking turns to nurse a little baby, so that the other one could rest.

What I came to understand until now is that the more a parent can love, accept and love her- or himself, choosing to be in a state of peace and happiness, the more they can love their children, and the more they are able to fulfill the child's needs for love and affection, creating an environment with sounds and energy of peace, play, joy and Love for the child to grow up in. I believe it is crucial, in order for the child to become a healthy, compassionate, authentic and sovereign human Being, that a child can grow up in a peaceful and psychologically/physically healthy environment where there is Love and kindness between the parents and in the larger household and environment, Love and kindness toward the child, and a deep understanding for the child's needs. This would be the ideal case.

For many of us, this wasn't the case though. Many of us grew up in distorted families and environments where there was aggression, anger, or fear and the energy of tension and disrespect. So, many of us – in order to feel safe at our individual level of need, built defense mechanisms around what didn't feel good, and grew into a different Being, a false Self, covering up the divine Source essence we always carry with us as our life force. Many of us suffered, were misunderstood, and bullied in school or later in corporate world, and for many of us this created a suffering to a point where we could no longer bear with this pain.

And yet, through our experiences and the related pain we felt, we re-learned, or rather remembered, that we are something so much bigger, vaster and brighter than we could ever imagine. Contrast is here to show us what we don't want, so that we can create what we do want. Recently, I heard this beautiful phrase: "It is easier to raise a happy child than to heal a broken adult." Yes, the goal would be to raise happy children in a world of love, peace, and community, even though, there always lies a treasure under where we stumble…

In my personal case, my suffering brought me to more awareness about who I truly am and what I am not. The pain that I thought I couldn't handle any longer, awakened me to my inner power that was always there. A power that was greater than any outside circumstances, because it came from the heart. And later in life, through meditation, Yoga, Qi Gong and other meditational practices I was able to release and transform ever more and more of those limited energy layers that were covering my light – and I am still going on with releasing…

Even though I am dreaming of a world where every baby is born through a loving conception into a loving and fully functioning happy family, a true support system, I came to understand that there was a reason I chose to grow up like this. Contrast is always making us more aware of what we don't want, hence guiding us toward what we do want. So in my case, I believe that I chose this kind of childhood to remember who I am inherently, and to remember what every human Being on this planet is and where we all come from. I learned and am still learning to become 'my own beloved'.

"You keep searching, hunting for the diamond necklace. Stop searching, for it is already around your neck." Rumi

I kept looking into the big blue eyes of this baby-boy, and my eyes smiled with deep love for this little whole Being. I stood there for a while and I talked to this beauty, welcoming him to this world. The baby's eyes responded in pure joy and well-being, it's body movements reflecting this pure joy, excitement, and Love. It's smile and excitement filled my heart with so much love and compassion, and I had tears in my eyes as I kept talking to him, lovingly smiling at him and showing my happy facial expressions. I felt an overwhelm of joy and gratefulness for this little miracle of life. I might have stood there for 5 min and then the mother came back. We exchanged some friendly words and then each of us went our own way. My heart felt recharged by this pure and loving interaction, and I couldn't help but seeing the wondrous miracle of life in everything for the rest of the day...

"You come to us from another world
From beyond the stars and void of space
Transcendent
Pure
Of unimaginable Beauty
Bringing with you the essence of Love.
You transform all who are touched by you
Mundane concerns, troubles, and sorrows dissolve in your presence
Bringing joy to ruler and ruled
To peasant and king.
You bewilder us with your grace.
All evils transform into goodness.
You are the master alchemist.
You light the fire of Love in Earth and Sky
In heart and soul of every being.
Through your love, existence and nonexistence merge.
All opposites unite.
All that is profane becomes sacred again." Rumi

When I first read this beautiful poem, the thought I had was of a little pure baby coming to Earth and carrying the Source essence visibly with it, and because this baby is peace and joy, it brings peace and joy to everyone, reuniting even those in dispute... these lines wonderfully describe the innocent purity of Gods Love.

Christmas is approaching, and with it the celebration of the birth of Jesus Christ, and here are some thoughts I'd like to share.

What most of us were taught, especially when I listen to Christmas carols, was that Jesus was holy, he was the Son of God, and some even consider him God. In the carols, it sounds like he was the only child of God that has ever been born (even though he himself said that every one is a child of God).

As I have already mentioned in this book, according to the channelings of Abraham, a group of spirit guides channeled by Esther Hicks, Jesus was no exception to the biological laws of recreation of humans, meaning that Mother Mary was no virgin in the physical, untouched sense, but conceived the child like every human being does, through sexual intercourse. This might come as a huge surprise to many, and it sure was for me when I first heard this particular channeling, for all I remember from the church teachings was that sex was a sin, it was dirty and punishable and so on. But what this truly means is that, while Mother Mary – through the eyes of those who wrote religion – was said to be a virgin, every other woman who conceived a child conceived it through sin... Imagine the suffering of these women... It was impossible to conceive without having committed a sin (today, there are ways of course), and so those women felt guilt, shame, and fear for what they had done, and might have even projected it onto their children... And the pure innocent child that would not know about the harsh judgment that it was produced through sin, wondered why it was treated unkind.

But what if all that wasn't true? What if beloved Mother Mary wasn't a virgin in the physical sense, and it was only the idea of those who misunderstood the divine feminine so to say, and created a lot of unnecessary suffering for every sacred women on Earth that became a mother?

So here is what I'd like to share about my thoughts of what the birth of Jesus truly meant, and maybe this is what God's message to the world truly is: Not only Jesus, but every baby is holy, for it carries the peace and purity of God, every baby is sacred, for every baby is a child of God. Every little newborn baby, be it girl or boy, be it black or white, red or yellow, poor or rich, comes directly from Source, from God, bringing with it divine peace, joy, and happiness. Every baby brings with it the seed of life planted in a beautiful divine perfect little body, enlightening its surroundings with this divine unconditional joy and purity. Look into a baby's eyes, and just let go for a while, smile in love into these eyes, and you will see God smiling back at you. In truth, every baby, every Being reflects God back to us -

"...you are reflecting a noble face..." (Rumi)

– yet where I believe we can feel it the most is in a baby girl or boy, for there are no programing's running yet, there is no layer of anything that covers the light of this precious Being. Yes, God is reflected in an adult's eyes, too, but there are most often veils already, fears of truly connecting, energetic barriers that this Being has built against love for self-protection. But a baby is just reflecting back to us the purity of alignment with Love and light, unlimited faith, and this blissful joy. If you look at a baby with unconditional Love, and allow your heart to open by this beautiful Being, this baby will reflect God's Love back to you, and so every baby is in a way a holy child of God, just like Jesus has shown us, for it comes from *life longing for itself...*

What babies are also teaching us is that we will never loose our true essence, the Source within, even though life will cause us to deviate from our paths due to the way we perceive the world around us. They show us that our experiences are a direct reflection of the vibrational frequency we are exuding, and they do this in a way that when you smile at them with Love, they will smile back at you. Yet when you look at them with anger or fear, they will reflect the same back to you by the expression in their faces, or they might even start crying. Similarly, in an environment of peace, a child will reflect the peace by being calm and easy. But if there is fear, anger, aggression in this environment, starting with the closest caregivers, the baby will be fearful and nervous, and it will probably cry a lot, because it does not feel safe... As if they felt that anything but Love is not our true nature and they respond to it in uneasy ways...

So, every baby is in a way an amazing teacher to show us that when we smile at the universe, the universe smiles back at us. When we look into the universe with anger or fear, then the universe will give more of it to us... All babies are our teachers, and I believe that every child of God and its parents are sacred and worthy of the same love and respect that the little boy Jesus and his parents received after he had been born.

Imagine for a moment that every baby would be welcomed by it's parents and the world like Jesus was. Imagine this baby would grow up knowing that it is holy, special, loved, beautiful, unique, that it is a child of God. Imagine this child would be loved and adored in its authentic uniqueness just like Jesus... Do you believe it is possible that, if we all grew up like this, we would all remember to only see Goodness in everyone, no matter who they might be or how they might behave? Do you think it is possible that we would all know about our healing power, the healing power of God inherently within us? Would it be possible that we are all creating a more peaceful world because we believe in Love, knowing we are special?

Every one of us, every single one, is born complete and beautiful. A miracle of Life, *"a manuscript of a divine letter" (Rumi).*

So often I hear that babies healed disputes in families where the most probably false selves or Ego's of a grand-parent or parent were battling to be right. So often I heard stories that little babies heal with their simple presence, for their presence is Love, peace, and innocence, and how depression or any other energetic miss-alignments that most often come from an abusive upbringing are suddenly dissolving. When I say that, I do not mean to blame any parent. My intention to write this chapter is to raise the consciousness of those that already are parents or those who want to be parents to understand that the way we treat ourselves is or will be the way we treat our children. And it will be the role model of how our children treat themselves and everyone else, including their own children, later in life. This is why it is so crucial to remember our divine essence as children of God, and for parents to also remember that their children are holy, and that they themselves are holy and whole as divine Beings, that every Mother is sacred just like Mother Mary.

When parents are still searching who they truly are, when they are still in fear, or when they are living according to any limited beliefs from their own childhood, then too often these limited beliefs get projected onto the child without or only little awareness. In other words, the child has to take the blame for an 'un-ready' mother/father. Projection means that the parent blames the child for something that isn't the baby's or child's fault, but the baby or child must take the blame for it, because the parent is unaware of that within her/himself.

Parents have a choice: Either choose to be in their divine Self, where she/he will recognize that the child reflects something back that actually needs attention and is in need to be healed within the parent, or to stay in the ego, in the false self that blames the child, the parent thinking that she or he is right, they know better, for they are older and more experienced and therefore knowing, and continue to argue or even punishing the child for whatever the parent overlooks within themselves. The child is feeling misunderstood and not heard, maybe even left alone with its feelings, and as a consequence, grows up thinking something is wrong with it, it is not worthy, it is not good enough, and so on.

Again, for almost everything, humans need a license, except for being a parent. Somehow the fact that everyone can be a parent is taken for granted on this world, no matter where they are on their journey back to spiritual enlightenment. And this might be true physically, but then so many still struggle with self-abuse and self-sabotage.

What a joy it would be to create parenting schools where every parent to be – girls and boys – who did not grow up knowing they are loved, special, unique, beautiful, etc., can learn to understand who they are first, where they learn to meditate, to become aware of their own wholeness and holiness as God-like Beings, where they understand themselves and learn to forgive and love themselves as much as everyone else, where they learn to take responsibility for how they feel and learn tools to get themselves back into a better feeling space, etc. I firmly believe that as the consciousness and awareness on this planet is rising, the importance of a loving upbringing for every child will no longer be disregarded, and children will be conceived consciously again.

I already see more and more pioneers out there trying to integrate this important awareness into schools and institutions, and I hope - and deep inside know - that, as we adults return to who we truly are – to Love, then the awareness of the importance of how to lovingly raise children into psychosocially and physically healthy Beings will expand as well.

I think it is important to understand that the child is a reflection of it's parents. What I observed over and over again, not only in my own Self, is that we take over the habits and beliefs of our parents which often results in the same physical ailments an – if not addressed and transformed – later in the same dis-eases. What we see, however, are not the genes of a child being dysfunctional, but rather the environment (micro to macro, parents and ancestors included), and the gene is only picking up on the vibrational messages of the environment, as proven by Dr. Bruce Lipton.

When I was a child, I could see these misalignments in my family and even the ailments they caused in my parents/sisters and myself. As an observer, I felt I was there to bring peace into this distortion, but I did not feel my voice to be heard. I picked up on energy around me, but whenever I wanted to help or do something to soothe (which is what children so often do, for they feel when their parents suffer), I was either being told to be quiet, or I was called a 'trouble-maker'.

I soon realized that I had to leave this unhealthy environment in order to be truly me, if I wanted to remain alive and sane. The environment I grew up in, where change, even positive change, was not really welcome, where the same destructive patterns kept repeating with no or only little awareness and openness to change, where the focus was on what's missing, and where complaining without changing was normal, while happiness and joy was abnormal, where my desperate attempts of re-aligning the dilemma were – sometimes even violently – opposed, would not be the environment for me to grow and expand into a healthy and fulfilled, happy human being. So I decided to leave at the age of 19, moving to Spain, just after graduating in Business Administration, hoping to live in a happier environment, hoping to 'find my tribe', and my truth, myself. Even though this sounds harsh, my Love for my parents is infinite. I know they have given what they could to raise my sisters, and me, and they did a great job based on their own awareness. One wise woman once said that the only job a parent has is to bring the soul, the child back to Earth, and to nourish it while it can't look after itself. This helped me to make peace with my experiences, and to forgive.

For many young parents, the only training or 'certification' they got is what had been role-modeled to them when they were children, whether this upbringing was in alignment with unconditional love and guidance or not.

The miraculous gift that little children are is often overseen by parents who were not truly ready to embrace the parent challenge yet, and so they are unable to see the miracle of life and the amazing possibilities to grow, to learn, to expand beyond their own limiting beliefs through the loving teachings of their children. Often, I heard the parent is right because she or he is older. Yet I learned that age has nothing to do with spiritual maturity, that spiritual maturity rather was a choice. And since it is not taught in school, many are unaware. Another notion I heard is that the child belongs to it's parents, and therefore, they can do with it whatever they want.

And yet, the child is coming to Earth as an ambassador of a *new world,* with an amplified awareness, for evolution continues constantly. I would even say that children come to certain families as healers to teach this family something important that could end a vicious cycle of a family pattern that has been going on for centuries.

I once heard a mother saying, even though she feels overwhelmed with her 7 children, that her children are her teachers. She realized through her daughters comment "Mom, just take a moment, just breathe, in through your nose, out of your mouth", that her daughter was teacher her that she is often in the future energetically and therefore anxious, instead of being in the present moment, when she is in peace and truly with her children. Because she feels under pressure when she is in the future (thinking of how she can accomplish all the chores), she cannot enjoy the time with her kids, and they will feel it, for a child will always feel the way it's mother feels. Not surprising it is then that the aftertaste that comes with this attitude for a parent is often guilt. And so this is a vicious cycle that will leave the child – depending on it's own level of sensitivity and the way it takes in those situations - often with a feeling that the child is rather a burden than a joy to it's parents.

"I am so small
I can barely be seen
How can this great love be inside me?
Look at your eyes
They are small
But they see enormous things." Rumi

Newborn life is such a miracle, such a joy… and I certainly hope that more and more parents choose wisely and understand what a blessing it is to put new life onto this Earth… Girl or boy, rich or poor, race, status, class… all of it doesn't matter. What matters is that every baby is sacred and deserves to be treated as such.

Just like I observe in nature… my wisest teacher: What a blessing a chickadee's nest this last spring in our garden was. To hear the little ones asking for food, to hear the satisfied and excited voices when the bird parent came with food. Any heart would open when it is confronted with a little baby, and even nature stories show how oftentimes animal mothers who would find human or other abandoned babies, would take them home and nourish them unconditionally. Just because they feel the unconditional love of a mother, they see the love there is in this newborn Being, and feel touched and nurture this beautiful baby until it is able to live on it's own. Besides, animals are great teachers showing humans that little ones need lots and lots of affection to be healthy on all levels. Only physical care, such as food is not enough. The child needs to be in the warm and peacefully loving energy of a responsive and affectionate parent to feel safe.

I always knew that I did not want to create life as long as I am not fully ready to embrace myself. I did not want to be a mother as long as I hadn't found that joy I felt in nature within myself, until I hadn't learned how to be the divine mother for myself. Deep inside, somehow I knew that whatever energy is still misaligned due to my upbringing or even past lives, it would show itself again when I have a child, for children reflect the parent's unhealed issues. And so my goal was to heal myself first and then – if I still feel the need - become a mother.

I believe that being a mother or father is the most responsible and important 'job' that exists other than living our life purpose. And that this job is way too underestimated. I have seen and am still seeing too many children that suffer for feeling misunderstood, for not being heard. I believe that, to heal this world by being a loving and guiding parent, it is crucial to understand who we truly are first in our own divine essence.

When we are in this space of Love, we will understand our children and we will be able to learn from them about how to create a world we love to live in.

To finish this chapter for now, I'd like to share some of Rumi's words that perfectly reflected my feelings while in High School:

"A strange passion is moving in my head.
My heart has become a bird
Which searches in the sky.
Every part of me goes in different directions
Is it really so
That the one I love is everywhere?" Rumi

And oftentimes, bored with the class content and in my own daydreams, when I looked outside, I would see a little blue opening of the sky, that seemed to be there just for me... And I felt loved, and it stirred my faith that there was something out there that loved me deeply just as I was....

7

God and Nature

As many of my dear readers might have noticed by now, I love mother Earth, I am in peace when I am in nature. Someone once called me 'nature's advocate'. Yes, the place I find silence and stillness is in nature, and throughout my life, silence became sacred to me. I would seek it in my travel-filled life, and I would often retreat from the busy city life, in order for me to feel balanced and connected again. If I could, I would choose to overnight at places outside of busy cities in nature. It almost became sacred to me to have a retreat where I can say 'so long' to the outside world, where I can just connect with myself. In these moments of stillness, I allow myself to go deep into my heart and feel… I would just *be and breathe.* I also learned other tools of feeling balanced, and would indulge in meditation, Qi Gong, Yoga or breathing exercises, and I would journal my feelings, my thoughts, and my questions arising – all of these activities, whenever possible, outdoors or with windows wide open. The only 'indoor' place I would go to just be is a Sauna. When I lived in Hong Kong, there was a Sauna for the residence of the high rise building we were living in, and every evening I would take an hour or so to go 'back into the womb', as I started to call my sacred Sauna time. It is in stillness that I would find and reconnect with myself, it is there where I found God as the Love in my heart.

"Silence is the language of God. All else is poor translation." Rumi

As you have already witnessed through my first chapters, the place where I have experienced God's truth the most was and still is in wilderness far away from humans and human-created noise. For some, this can even be a moment with their pets or a baby or a toddler. The point here is to just be immersed in an unconditionally loving energy, beyond judgment and duality. Be it at a beach, a forest, a meadow, or just behind a building in a backyard with some plants and a fountain, whenever silence and stillness is surrounding me, I can hear God's voice, for I hear myself, my innermost feelings, my intuition. In this space, I would not only become aware of my own barriers I built against Love, but also I would be able to hear, to *feel*, ideas or inspirations guiding me in my life.

I have learned to allow myself to be with all my feelings, and just lovingly sitting with them, like I would sit with beloved friends. What do they tell me? Where do they guide me? What pains or blockages am I experiencing in my energy field, when there is only love and peace surrounding me? What barriers have I built to protect myself from the world or other people, or from Love? Where does my body have tensions and what do these tensions indicate?

When I am alone in the peace and joy of nature, not focused on doing, but just being, I can go so much deeper to fulfill Rumi's sacred assignment…

"Your task is not to seek for love, but merely to seek and find all the barriers within yourself that you have built against it."

We are God, and God is Love. We are divine Beings of Love and Light. This is what is our essence. The limiting belief systems we created around our experiences, the barriers are in a way layers that are shadowing our divine essence, our Light, which is beautifully shown in the 'Story of the Golden Buddha'. I love this story so much, for it perfectly explains who we are:

'Once there was clay Buddha found in a jungle, and the Buddhist monks who found it loved the statue and made it part of their family. But soon they were threatened and had to leave the site. They took the Buddha with them. On the road, the clay began to crack and chip off from the statue. One night, the guardian monk shone onto the statue to check if everything was ok, and a strong golden light was reflected back to him. He called the other monks, and together, they started to investigate and realized that the clay started to chip off from the statue all over, and it seemed like it was covering another essence underneath. So they started to take off all the clay. The more they took, the more a beautiful Golden statue came to sight, until they saw this beautiful golden Buddha, that had been covered in layers and layers of protection all over these years.'

I truly believe that this story illustrates perfectly who we as human Beings are, Beings of pure light. However, energy imprints that we have experienced over our live times here on Earth and in early childhood have left their trace, and in response, we have created these defense barriers in order to protect ourselves from whatever we experienced. These defense barriers can be seen as layers of misaligned energy, or clay, that can shadow our light. Remember, we come to Earth as pure God essence, shining our light freely, inspiring and being who we truly are.

And then, we built barriers against love, layers of clay, feeling that we need to protect ourselves from this world. So, how do we get back to this Golden essence within all of us?

The answer is as simple as it is difficult: 'By remembering who we truly are, being in silence and removing all these 'clay' layers as we become aware of them and how they have inhibited us to shine our truest light. Walking the Earth as love and peace, as kindness and sincerity, with ourselves and everyone we meet.

Nature provided a safe haven for me to get to know myself as *Love being my religion, and every loving heart being my temple.* In these moments of silence and stillness in nature, when I am one with the divine feminine, this unconditional love, and the divine masculine, structure, form and divine order in nature, both nourishing each other equally and harmoniously, I can find clarity about my own energetic barriers.

I am grateful for every barrier that shows up, and often they make themselves known through tightness in my body, or negative feelings of any sort. And when I find and embrace them, and ask them what they are here to teach me, I would always find answers through feelings. I truly believe that this is how we heal. For me, I take on the non-judgmental Love of our environment, the trees, birds, waters, etc., and allow them to guide me home. In other words, I allow them to help me finding the barriers I've built that might no longer serve me, and release and replace them with thoughts and feelings that actually are serving me and everyone, kind of like releasing the clay of the Golden Buddha.

When I am in nature far away from people, there is nothing I need to protect myself from; all I feel is this all embracing Love. I love the multidimensional openness as I observe and integrate my feelings, transcending the barriers that want to be known at this point, with the loving assistance of a waterfall or the wisdom of an old tree, listening to what my heart is telling me, and floating home closer into my heart, to Love, to God.

And when I watch and observe wildlife – a hawk right above my head, gently screaming, and soaring high up in the sky in a spiral form, or ants busy and organized, or birds enjoying the day and praising the light with their joyful songs – I can't help but be happy. I see truth in all of this, in this moment… nature is always bringing me back to that precious moment, to the here and now. And in this moment, when I hear the peaceful chirping of my friends, the birds, I am just happy. I allow all of this in, the fresh sparkling air, the gentle green of trees, the flow of a waterfall down the mountain, the peace of this moment – I am allowing all of it into my body and Being, filling me with new life force, with new energy, with faith… and I feel home within my heart.

You see, we humans have learned to somehow not listen to our innermost feelings. We have learned to always be busy, and even when we are not busy, most of us distract ourselves from being in stillness and rather entertain ourselves by watching TV or engaging in any other distractive behaviors…. So why are we doing that? Are we afraid to feel who we truly are? Are we afraid of the pain we might feel when we remember harsh experiences? Are we afraid to feel that we are Love, that we are God? But if we are God, why are we afraid?

Again, the answer I found is in nature… Let it be… Earth is an amazing teacher. The best words to describe how I feel with my beloved Earth are (Earth speaking): *'I don't teach. I love. Love teaches.'*

The green forests, the infinite oceans with their colorful wildlife, the variety of flowers and animals, birds and butterflies on the surface of Earth, the amazing crystals reflecting Earth's inner beauty, the beautiful beaches, waterfalls and rivers… When I am in nature, I am often just in awe about the gift of Being that she teaches me: for example, watching the seasons go bye from the moment when the trees start to have blossoms and tiny green leaves to the moment where they carry fruit, to the season when grown leaves turn into yellow, orange and red colors and fall down to the ground… I find Rumi's truth here – *to remain alive, die in Love…* A tree obviously has learned to let 'old energy' fall of it, including it's fruits and leaves, it is perfectly wise and knows what to do. So why don't humans respect this divinity of a wise tree and trim it until it can't grow new branches any longer and would die?

Here is a quote I heard once that deeply resonated:

"Man is the most insane species. He worships an invisible God and slaughters a visible Nature, without realizing that this visible Nature he slaughters is the invisible God he worships." (Hubert Reeves)

Is the misunderstanding of humans of nature and the abuse of her just a reflection of the abuse those people do with themselves by not living from their innermost God-like essence, but from a limited ego space where they feel the need to force power or beliefs onto other Beings, including trees, flowers, animals, or entire landscapes? Would the remembrance of who they truly are finally put an end to this insanity, so that the beauty and perfection of nature – without human interference – could be preserved not only for it's own sake and the health of all creation living with it (for I believe our health is a reflection of also the nature environment we live in), but for all future generations to come?

As shown, everything starts within us, so to put and end to the destruction and exploitation of our sacred mother Earth we need to remember who we truly are, and when we do, I believe we will finally be able to heal the separation from everyone and everything, including Earth. Maybe, when humankind realizes that it is not what eyes can see, but so much more... we will then realize that we are Source energy incarnated in a physical body, divine feminine and divine masculine (as represented in Earth) at the same time. Have you ever asked yourself why one half of your body looks like the other? Why do you have two sides within you, two brain hemispheres, right and left, two arms, two legs, etc.? Many studies today show that when people generally have ailments on the left side of their bodies, there is a misalignment with the divine feminine, while if the ailments occur on the right side of the body, this could be a sign of the divine masculine being out of alignment... is it the war of the divine feminine and the divine masculine within us that is reflected in how we treat the Earth?

It is happening more and more as humanity awakens, but it still seems difficult for humans to understand that they are divine creators, powerful spiritual Beings that are having a physical experience. So many still believe that we are physical Beings having a spiritual experience, but this is kind of thinking backwards. It is like saying 'wings do have birds', rather than 'birds do have wings'.

I believe so many of us are aware now of systems that are no longer supporting a healthy, connected and growing humanity, but are only profit-minded, and keep humans enslaved. And I believe that I am not alone to feel the urge that this needs to change. And it changes with us. As we remember and align with our truth again, we can transform this world into a place of love and peace, and turn everything we've built that is no longer supporting Love and Life on this planet can be recreated into something that does.

But we need to start within ourselves to do that, we need to let go of our very own barriers we've built against love, and that is why I wanted to write this chapter about nature. Nature has and is helping me to *'be the change I want to see in this world' (Gandhi).*

When we start to release all those energetic blockages against love, and become love again, we will be able to bring back the light and peace that this planet, and all creation, so desperately deserves. Nature never judges. Nature just accepts and loves unconditionally. Nature *is* the reflection of God's noble face, just as we are.

"Be like melting snow – wash yourself of yourself. Beauty surrounds us." Rumi

In other words,' *release the barriers you have built against Love...'*

Here is something else in this context that I'd like to share. Again, nature taught me this: Every year in spring time, no matter where I am in the world, wherever there is green ground and trees, a beautiful symphony of bird songs would wake me up in the mornings... What more divine way exists to wake us up than then voices of hundreds of birds all singing their song, all singing their music, in a perfect harmonious symphony of pure bliss and joy....

Imagine humankind would do this. What I learn from this is that we are all divine Beings, coming from the same Source, we all are an individualized expression of God: humans, animals, birds, trees, flowers... We are all having our own unique skills and talents, our own qualities and wonders. Nature is showing is that it is divine order for every being, every bird, to sing our own song, to share with the world our authentic Being. In this world that was created, we are, however, conditioned to all fit in the same scheme: Once we go to school, we learn about science, we are told that we need to get good degrees in order to get a good title in order to get a well paid job. We do not learn, however, the most important science: How to "sing our own song and live a happy and fulfilled live doing that".

The concert of songbirds is the perfect example: Imagine every bird trying to be like a, let's say, a pigeon. Every bird is conditioned to sing the song of the pigeon: Gruuuhgruuuu- gruuuugruuuu. And now imagine waking up to a beautiful spring day, only hearing birds that are trying to sing this one song of the pigeon…, trying hard for it is not it's nature to sing this way, but the birds keeps trying because they must by a worlds that demands conformity… Eventually, this poor bird will burn out and be quit and maybe even die, for it feels like it has lost it's power…

So mother Earth was and is teaching us all along the way that if we just open up and listen again, we will become whole and complete, we will return from a disconnected space of trying to sing like a pigeon to the holy wholeness of who we truly are, singing our very own song. All we need to do is to embrace variety, just like nature is showing us.

Another beautiful example of what nature is teaching us is the transformation from a caterpillar into a butterfly: Imagine a caterpillar, it has inherently everything it needs to become a beautiful butterfly. When the caterpillar feels it is time, guided by the divine voice within, it goes into a cocoon (kind of like a retreat in nature), spending time in silence, and taking time to transform to become the most beautiful version of itself — all of this happens in the stillness of the cocoon. Then, after a certain time, the now fully developed butterfly starts to bend and twist and move inside the cocoon, for it has become too small for the butterfly to feel free (similar to limited beliefs and ego based ways of living, or the old structure of the world that had been created), as it is ready now to spread it's wings and fly as this beautiful colorful Being it truly is, into a new perspective of life, a new view, ready to explore life from all angles of seeing… And let's not forget, by the butterfly joyfully being who it is, it brings joy and bliss and awe to anyone who see's it…

"You were born with wings. Why prefer to crawl through life?" Rumi

Could this be a metaphor from our greatest teacher, Earth, for an awakening humanity, too? Similar, there is the snake that shows us that when her skin has become to small for her to live in, she sheds the old skin and grows into a greater Being…

I think you get the point. Nature is indeed my greatest teacher, and so the more we preserve her beauty, the more we respect her and her teachings, the more we are seeking her presence in our lives, the more we will remember who we are.

8

God and Thought

"Be empty of worrying.
Think of who created thought!
Why do you stay in prison
When the door is so wide open?" *Rumi*

In the beginning of everything, there was a thought, an idea. Merely all of what we see manifested from that place, including the world and all the systems humankind has created, stem from a thought, an idea. What this shows us is that the power of thought can be used to create a new world, too, a peaceful and thriving world we are all longing for.

"Everything you possess of skill, and wealth, and handicraft, wasn't it first merely a thought and a quest?" *Rumi*

Buddhists already knew that 'we are what we think', as much as Jesus was preaching this principle truth. There are many wisdom traditions in the world that teach the power of thought, how they influence our lives, and how important it is to cultivate positive thoughts and a peaceful mindset. Modern scientific studies, especially from Dr. Bruce Lipton, show the power of thought also in situations of a late-stage illness of the body. I believe my father, because he believed his doctor, who told him that he had 3 weeks to live, left us this early because the power of his thought made him do so. I remember how my step-mom told me that he died during 3 days, always waking up again, as if he knew that it was the thought making him go and that he actually had a choice… (bless his beautiful soul).

I believe that once we find our inherent connection to God, we will handle our thoughts in a different way, remembering that we are not our thoughts, but remembering that we always have a choice how or what to think. So, in order to heal ourselves from the illusion of separation, how do we shift our thoughts?

"Put your thoughts to sleep.
Do not let them cast a shadow
Over the moon of your heart.
Let go of thinking.
The moon shines brighter when it doesn't avoid the night." *Rumi*

What powerful lines, they kept me pondering about for quite a while. Usually, I go with my first hit, and this is how I felt:

Thoughts can create the life of our dreams, or they can create the life we are most afraid of - kind of like discussed earlier in the idea of heaven and hell. Thoughts can also create anything in between, because 'where your thought goes, energy flows'.

The Law of Attraction, a universal principle that is very much connected to our thoughts, is like gravity, it works whether you are aware of it or not, whether we think deliberately or by default. So, if our thoughts are aligned with the life of our dreams, our emotions will respond to them in a positive, excited anticipating way, and it won't take long until the physical manifestation follows, because thought creates feeling, feeling creates vibrational frequency, and it is our vibrational frequency that life becomes the mirror of. This is also true for thoughts that are not aligned, which are followed by tight or negative feelings, that can turn into energetic blockages in our bodies, and if continued to be ignored, into physical ailments.

"Whether you think you can do it, or you think you can't, you are right." Henry Ford

Our thoughts, conscious or unconscious (meaning those thoughts that run in our sub- or unconscious mind, thoughts we are not aware of but that are reflected in our vibrational frequency) have power. And this power manifests into physical matter. The vision we have already exists in another dimension, and manifestation is only a matter of how intensely we feel this vision in our vibration.

Thoughts influence every level and dimension of our lives, and this is widely know by now. They create health, or dis-ease, they create inner peace or turmoil. They create connection or division; they create love, or hatred. They create empowerment or anxiety. They create war, or peace. They create happiness or frustration. Thoughts are responsible for either free flowing energy or disrupted energy, for thoughts have energy and therefore create feelings.

We as vibrational energetic Beings come from pure Love and Joy. This is our divine heritage, our true Being, our home vibration, so to speak. If our thoughts are aligned with our 'home vibration' (pure bliss, as can be seen in a happy baby), our energy and vibration feels light and joyful, and life seems to easily and effortlessly flow, bringing to us what we desire. If our thoughts are in any way limited due to the conditioning we went through on this planet as children, our energy, as a result, becomes disrupted due to our limited beliefs and can create –if not addressed - ailments and later dis-eases. Oftentimes, dis-eases can bring a new awareness to people in terms of new, self-serving thoughts that will then create happier and more peaceful emotions and vibrant health again. So many people are known by today who went through critical late-stage diseases, and were able to transform whatever thoughts and feelings were behind this 'wake-up-call, living healthy and happy today…

Yet to become aware of any thoughts that are not in alignment can be a challenge. The way I learned to find out what my thoughts are was and still is to deeply listening to my feelings (in nature, for example), for they will always guide us to our thoughts. Whenever you feel tightness in your body, here is an exercise I do regularly to help myself, which will only take you two minutes (of course, you can do it with more time, whatever suits you). Remember that this exercise is loving sharing of the author, who helped herself, but who is not a doctor. If you have any physical ailment or disease you are trying to heal, please consult a doctor or practitioner of your choice. The author is in no way responsible for any outcomes of this exercise.

Sit down with your spine straight and upright (this creates a healthy flow of energy) and close your eyes. Your feet are flat on the floor, your hands rest in your lap, nothing is crossed. Shut down your mind; feel as if you switch 'the light off' in your head, so your mind becomes blank and you stop thinking. Take a deep breath, inhaling golden, diamond sparkling light and have it fill your entire body and energy field, scanning your body for anything that feels tight, scanning for any denser, darker area. If you detect a place in your body that kind of feels closed/off/tight, feel into it, breathing more golden light into this place. Ask it gently what message it contains for you and just listen, embracing this area and breathing in all your love. Listen to what is coming up... words, colors, pictures or even a message... Listen to all that's coming up for you, just have your heart speak to you along with this dense area in your body. Journal whatever thoughts are coming up for you, write it gently down, staying in this aligned space with your physical body. Thank the area for teaching you whatever limited thought/belief might be behind it, and visualize the golden light you keep breathing into this area slowly dissipate the dense energy. Embrace yourself, love your body. When you feel lighter and like the density is no longer there, bring yourself gently back into this present moment.

Remember your body is your best friend during your incarnation. It serves you so you can enjoy the beauty of this incarnation – if you choose to see it, of course. Take care of it. Respect it's needs, and stop any self-abuse now, like smoking, drinking, eating processed non-organic foods and sugar, and so on.

I believe a big part of our connection back to ourselves, to God, is to 'purify' our entire system, the mental, emotional, and physical body from any toxic energy, chemicals, and foods. When I did this myself, when I gradually detoxified my body and Being (and I am still giving in sometimes, especially for chocolate), my ability to truly listen to the voice within became much more refined. And, just a while ago, I found a chocolate that still melts on your tongue, but is 100% cacao and contains no sugar☺. But back to the power of our thoughts...

What I learned is that we operate this way: The messages we have been given when we were little children usually create a response within us, and this response is often that we would feel bad about what our parents or other people criticized about us, because inherently we want to be loved and included. In other words, those very things become our shadows, we begin to suppress them in order to be loved and nourished. It can also be that for example you have very angry parent. As you watch what this causes in the family, like for example passive aggression, tension or uneasy feelings, fear, or choleric outbreaks because of a tiny reason, you might begin to tell yourself that you will never be angry, so you begin to suppress or deny any angry feeling. In a person that seems to be controlled by anger, this anger somehow got stifled, meaning that the person rejects or suppresses this emotion on order to 'be loved' or because of the way it grew up thinks that 'anger is not a good thing' or 'anger creates bad situations or disharmony in a family and therefore has no place', whatever the thought behind it is. This was my case. But by avoiding to feel emotions, they don't go away, the contrary. They will show up over and over again, until we can lovingly embrace them as parts of ourselves that need to be loved like all our good traits, too. I learned to become friends with my latent anger, I embraced it like a little crying baby that needed to be held and soothed and loved. And by doing this, I realized that I could use the loving power of this emotion to create what I want. Many people use sports or engaging in creative activity, which can also help if you have stagnant anger. For me, however, to just lovingly embrace this inner anger like a little crying child, having compassion with this rejected part of myself, holding and lovingly accepting it, meant to transform and release it. You can do this with any other emotion that feels uncomfortable, too.

How do you find out whether you are holding any negative suppressed emotions within yourself? Well, here is what I learned:

What others say or do is always a reflection of them, and not of you. In Rumi's words:

"The beauty you see in my is a reflection of you." Rumi

Not only is the beauty we see in others a reflection of us, but also what we are avoiding to see in us. When you find yourself judging others because they are, for example, impatient, angry, fearful or whatever, this is also a reflection of you, and the fact that you see it in others is your awareness of that, and if that awareness is there, it means you have or are this very trait you see in others. This is how the loving universe is reminding us to embrace our shadows. To go deeper into this subject, Debbie Ford wrote a wonderful book, "The dark side of the light chasers", which explains perfectly what dynamics are happening there. But to keep it short, we see and judge in others what we avoid seeing in ourselves. So, when we find ourselves judging others, it is a perfect moment to become aware what we need to lovingly accept about ourselves. For that, the exercises shared earlier can help.

Once we truly become aware of all that we are and lovingly accept all that we are, the seemingly good and bad traits, we are indeed coming home to ourselves, to God. Where there is Love, there is God. So love yourself unconditionally, and program yourself with thoughts that support you in that. This way, you are healing the victim and become the empowered creator of your life.

Thoughts are powerful. Thoughts are truly who we are, and so, by changing our thoughts, we are constantly able to change ourselves or anything, including the world. Wayne Dyer said it beautifully: When we change the way we look at things, the things we look at change." Or, in Eckhart Tolle's words: "The primary cause of unhappiness is never the situation itself but our thoughts about it." So, make sure that your thoughts are in alignment with Love always and you will remain in being a deliberate creator. Have you ever noticed that people who fully accept and love themselves always see something positive in others or situations? It is only a reflection of them... And have you ever noticed that those who always see something good in others, are in general healthier and happier people? This is what happens when we become aware and remember who we truly are, which is Love. As Rumi said, when we release the barriers we have built against the Love, when we love 'our neighbor as we love ourselves, in other words, we see the Love we are in our neighbor, too, it is then that we have returned home. But we need to start within ourselves. If you try to fix the separation from the outside, trying to love others, while you are still in war with yourself, it won't work.

Remember that whenever you are in your natural state of Being, which pure Love and Bliss, you will feel good. When you don't feel good, there is something within you, a misaligned emotion stemming from a thought that's not I alignment with who you truly are. Find this thought and lovingly heal it with the exercises shared.

You can also coach yourself in a way that "... it is safe for me to feel this way..." or whatever would be an affirmation that enables and empowers you to feel a feeling that keeps coming up, because it wants to be lovingly accepted as part of you, and you are Love. We can heal our entire experience in this world by being gentle and kind with our emotions and our thoughts, knowing that the two go hand in hand. And when you do this, when you become your own best friend, your own ally – for God dwells within you, as you -, you will be able to live Life fully and passionately again, feeling the Love that is everywhere for you!

"Look past your thoughts, so you may drink the pure nectar of This Moment." Rumi

9

God and Purpose

Have you ever noticed that when you force yourself to do something that doesn't bring you joy, you struggle. You feel resistance, like paddling against the current, of not wanting to do it. This is when you are going against this unconditionally loving life force that gently nudges you towards your purpose, and your purpose on this planet always has to do with something that brings you deep fulfillment and joy. When you get an inspiration, a divine idea that would serve way more people, and you start pursuing it, not really knowing even how to bring it into reality, you feel like the universe has your back and brings to you people, opportunities, and other ideas for actions and steps to move towards your goal, your divine idea. You feel at ease, in the flow, joyful and relaxed, excited and passionate about what you are doing. This is when we are putting ourselves into alignment with God, our true essence within, and since we all are an individual expression of Source energy, everything flows easily without obstacles. If there are obstacles while we are living our purpose in alignment with God, the universe will usually solve them fast. This is how I feel in this moment, writing this book that I hope serves all of you beautiful souls wandering on this planet trying to find the truth. I truly hope that this book brings you closer to your divine essence. My hope is that it inspires you to return home to your own heart, to God, which is who you truly are.

I often have been asking myself: What is my purpose in this lifetime? What is my mission on this planet? Why am I truly here? What is it about me that I can share with others that no one else has? How can I serve people that are also seeking for the truth? Here is one thing I learned:

"What you seek
Is seeking you". Rumi

I interpret this quote in way that what we love to do will always come back to us, no matter how much we neglected it. We all have hobbies, things we love to do because they bring us joy, they put us 'into the zone', whether we are living them or not. But often we are told "You can't make a living out of ....". Yet, many people tried, and the best singers are those who love to sing. The best painters are those who love to paint. The best Coaches are those who love to empower others, etc. I came to understand this quote as 'do what brings you joy, for this is who you truly are and – being and living what brings you joy joyfully – this is how you will enlighten the world.' When we do what we love, even though we just start it as a side business, or as a hobby, we will also re-align with this magnificent God essence within us. We are the *love of the beloved,* and when we allow ourselves to do what we love again, we will become more of what we truly are, pure Joy, Love and Bliss, in other words, God.

I never truly believed that we came to Earth to only live a monotonous life, get a degree, get a job, and pay taxes. A life in which we do a job that doesn't fulfill us because we can't live our full range of talents and skills, from 9 – 5, Monday till Friday, waiting for the weekends where we would be 'allowed' to do what truly brings us joy… longing for our holidays where we would finally have time to chill out or travel…

This is how I started 27 years ago, and travelling has always been important to me. Somehow travelling meant expansion to me, it meant freedom… So I tried to find a way to make travelling my profession, and became an Airline flight attendant. Although I certainly liked the travelling part, this profession came with other things that made life not so comfortable. So, after 6 years in the air, I looked further, still asking myself the same questions. I was still feeling the need to fit into this world, and I thought there must be a profession that really makes me happy…

When I look at this today, I have a smile on my face, knowing that something beautiful was happening. That the jobs which are known and named until now are only a small fraction of what is truly possible. I can feel and see that the more and more people become empowered to be who they truly are, the more they will *create* professions that match their potential, their unique skills and abilities. The greatest thing about these new professions, including spiritual, transformational Coaching and Speaking, which is what I do today, is that they help everyone, they truly *serve* people. You are no longer working your butt off for somebody, but you apply your unique skills and talents to help people feeling more alive so that ultimately we all live a happier life. And the happier people are, the happier we all and our Earth will be, because happiness is contagious and invigorating. When we do what we love, we will be an inspiration for everyone we meet. We will be the expansion God so desires, for Life longs for Life, and Love longs for Love just as much as we long to be ourselves, for we are Love and Life – or God, whether we are aware of it or not.

And God knows I tried many different areas before deciding what truly makes me happy: From Fashion design to Business Administration, from Aviation to Beauty Business, from Color and Fashion style consultant to Psychology … It was only when I started studying Spirituality… that I finally found truth and home. Why? Because I have a better understanding now of who I am and continue to learn and expand in all my divine vastness, power and beauty. I am Love that is not bound on what degree I have, or how I look like or how I behave, it is not bound on wealth nor status… all these illusions of this world I could finally transcend because I feel this true, unconditional Love that I am and every reader is.

"'How shall I help the world?' 'By understanding it.' 'How shall I understand it?' 'By turning away from it.' 'How then shall I serve humanity?' 'By understanding yourself.'" Rumi

When I found this beautiful poem and thought about it, I realized that my inner voice had already guided me to do this for a long time in my own way. About 20 years ago, I stopped listening to radio and TV news and advertisements. I felt that the 'news' were only heartbreaking and fear instilling messages, while advertising made you feel like you needed something in order to be healthy or 'in' or whatever, it nourished the belief 'I am not good enough as long as I don't have this or that'. Later, when advertisements were coming in without 'warning', I refused to even turn the radio on, until I found channels that were Listener sponsored and did not contain advertisement or news. I decided to see the beautiful things that were not mentioned in the news, for I believed that for every bad news there is at least 10 good news. Back then, I also stopped watching TV, and even quit my favorite 'drama' soap I had followed many years, wondering how the actors appeared to look younger with every new episode, even after many years. I had put my back on all of these 'distractions' in order to find out more about life and myself, beyond my body, gender, age, orientation, or interest, beyond the systems of this world.

I know today that by doing this I had given myself one the biggest gifts to get to truly know myself. And what a gift it is to better understand myself. I learned so many things through this process, for example where my own personal boundaries are, what I can tolerate, if my behavior was in alignment with my own needs, but most importantly what truly brings me true joy. And what brings me joy is to see happy and lovingly empowered people. So I started asking myself: How can I help create more happy people? And this is when I started my journey of self-employment in order to help people find out who they are and what brings them joy.

"Let yourself be silently drawn by the stronger pull of what you really love." "Let the beauty of what we love be what we do." Rumi

We already know what our purpose is, since it is always something that brings us deep joy and fulfillment. It can be anything. I recently heart someone saying that this world, as it is ascending into 5th dimension, will have a whole lot of 'new' creative jobs that have not yet existed in it's form until now. The only question we need to ask ourselves is: What is it that brings *me* joy? What was my hobby when I was little, something I truly loved doing, what brought me pure bliss?

"You only live once. If you don't go for your dream, who will? Live today with passion." Rumi

How do we get to know what brings us true joy, if we have forgotten? I once heard a speaker asking the people in the audience what they do that brings them joy? One man raised his had and said 'singing'. So the speaker invited him to sing for the audience. The man began shy and insecure, but you could hear that his voice was beautiful and had power. Then the speaker told him: 'Imagine this would be your last day, and you would die tonight. How would you sing?' The man hesitated for a while, obviously shocked by this question. And suddenly, he began to sing full chest... the full potential of his voice started to vibrate the entire room, and I am sure it gave every one in the audience goose bumps... including myself, and I was not even physically there but on my lap top...

Rumi's words *"Live today with passion"* teach us again to truly live in the moment and do what we love full-heartedly, without thinking about other people's opinions, for the most destructive and self-abusive behavior we could ever display is to believe what other's think about us, what other people's opinion is about us. Why? Because what other people think, is a reflection of them and not of you. Maybe they – if they judge you – still are in fear of living who they truly are? The only path we can align with to inspire and truly help them to find their own God-essence within is to walk our path, to do what brings us joy fully! Because if people see you doing this, if you live the inspired life, that's when they will start thinking... 'oh, if she or he can do it, so can I'. So start walking your path without fear, and as I said, even though you start it as a side business and keep your job if you have one to pay your bills, start doing what you love, and do it with all your Love and passion! Remember...

As you start to walk the way, the way appears. Rumi

So, if you can, try to retreat from your ego who needs to have it all figured out, who needs to have all the details, outcomes and possible dangers in order to start something new, and just listen to your heart that will guide as you start doing what makes you feel alive, what brings bliss and joy into your Being, what makes you wake up in the morning early because you can't wait to start the day doing what you love… You might say – how is this done if I have chores to do, children to nourish, work to do, etc. Well, start by taking maybe 30 min or an hour, making sure that your kids are well looked after, setting all that can wait aside, and diligently giving yourself a couple of min each day doing what you love.

I heard this saying once: Ego says 'before you jump, look where the ground is and double check that the parachute is functioning perfectly well.' Spirit says 'Jump, and let your wings grow on the way.' I would certainly not take that literally, but I believe that this is what Rumi meant by saying "As you start walking the way, the way will appear." So, even though you start by stealing one half hour away from your busy life, you might be surprised what is growing out of it… So have fun getting started doing passionately what you love. I certainly enjoy the unfolding of the path as I am doing what I love, and I want to share a last quote in this context with you that helped me a lot on my path:

"Courage is a love affair with the unknown." Osho

Shine your light, beloved Soul, sing your music, create what is truly your hearts calling, and live in trust and faith that the universe will support you in every step. Imagine the people on this planet, each living what brings them joy, and by doing *their* work, serving others. It would sound like the beautiful song bird symphony I hear every spring time… Oh how wonderful this world will be once we all truly live the courage to be ourselves. The highest and deepest expression of ourselves… we will transcend time lines, density, suffering and all the other 'old world' bounded conditions. Oh what a world this could be☺!

10

God and Death

I would like to explore about this subject, because many people are still deeply afraid of death, thinking that when our physical bodies die, than this is the end. But if we are God, and God is infinite, aren't we infinite, too? At this point, let me share this beautiful Death poem by Mary Elizabeth Frye, which I shared on the day of the funeral of my father 3 years ago:

Do not stand at my grave and weep
I am not there; I do not sleep.
I am a thousand winds that blow,
I am the diamond glints on snow,
I am the sun on ripened grain,
I am the gentle autumn rain.
When you awaken in the morning's hush
I am the swift uplifting rush
Of quiet birds in circled flight.
I am the soft stars that shine at night.
Do not stand at my grave and cry,
I am not there; I did not die.

I remember to be deeply afraid of death when I was a little child. Seeing a human skeleton gave me the chills, and when I needed to go to the restroom at night in the dark, I was afraid to see a skeleton… Still in my teenage years when I was taught about the human body in Biology, I felt haunted by the sight of a skeleton. Yet even though I felt afraid, something fascinated me about it. I had not heard until then that we humans could actually have many life times if we choose so, in fact, the culture I grew up in believed that this life is all we have. So I started to seek for evidence, because something inside of me was sure that I did not walk this Earth for the first time.

Then, when I learned about the Teachings of Buddha, I was introduced to the concept of re-incarnation. The explanations about us being souls that have a physical body experience so that our consciousness could grow and expand made complete sense to me, so much more sense than the belief that we only have one lifetime, and that the death of the physical body is the end of our life in general.

So here I was with two different ideas that needed research and exploration. As I said, Buddha's teachings resonated much more with me; in fact, somewhere in my heart I knew this was true. Where in the world would those old fears come from otherwise? Or why did I remember certain places on this planet in detail – colors, smells, shapes, and forms, even though I had never visited them in this life time before? Why – if I looked into the eyes of certain people – did I feel like I knew them, I knew their soul, even though it was the first time we met in this lifetime?

All these questions led me to go even deeper. I was determined to find the truth. At that time, my research also led me to how the Holy Bible had been changed by those in charge, or 'in power' back then. According to my research, the concept of reincarnation, amongst other concepts that were originally included, were taken out of the bible, because they were too empowering to humans. I was shocked when I understood the extend of suffering and fear the removal of these originally included concepts from the bible must have created in people back then, all over those years, and still today.

"This place is a dream. Only a sleeper considers it real. Then death comes like dawn, and you wake up laughing at what you thought was your grief." Rumi

When I remember my teenage and early adult years, the believe that there must be something other than this life time, something way bigger and vaster, a deeper sense of all, of my life, my thoughts, my own suffering, my own joy, kept me alive and made me not give up.

Later in College, I remember one of my Professors whom I deeply respected. He came into class one day, the class quieted down and he said: 'Forget everything you know. Just know this: *You are God.*'

In his class, I was introduced to a Native Mexican tribe, the Yaqui, which believed that Death is their best friend, always being on their left shoulder. At first, I got chills, but then I understood the meaning: If death is our best friend, and we live every day, every moment like our last, and because we live in the moment rather than in the past or in the future, wouldn't life be much more meaningful? Wouldn't we make our choices and our decisions wiser? Wouldn't we start living our lives with passion, doing what fulfills us? Wouldn't we start thinking in a different way, in a way that makes every human interaction precious, if we can bless it and share with love, knowing who we truly are? Wouldn't we just *be* Love and give Love unconditionally? But most of all, would we *remember* who we truly are, beyond all the illusions we were taught?

Whenever something is transitioning, meaning the physical part of it is left without the life force that was breathing through it, we call it death. I'd even say, death is a language term of a humanity not truly understanding that everything is energy, and that consciousness continues, it just *is*. So death is rather a dimensional change, a change from 3D back to the infinite, where our consciousness exists as pure bliss, until we – if we do so - choose to reincarnate again. So, when a living Being transitions back from perceived 3-Dimensionality into Multidimensionality, it might be the end for this body, this hair, this skin in this physical incarnation, but it is a new beginning, a returning home into the Infinite of the soul that lived the body.

"I am not this hair. I am not this skin. I am the soul that lives within. Our Death is our wedding with eternity." Rumi

With these words I choose to finish my first book. The second one will follow soon, and with it, we shall explore the connection between God, or Love, with other subjects or even deeper with the subjects in this book.

My wish and my hope for my beloved readers is that this book empowers you, allows you to grow your wings and live your life in it's truest and deepest joy as the powerful creator that you truly are! Because remember…

"You were born with wings. Why prefer to crawl though life?" Rumi

Thank you for this beautiful, amazing, and loving Being that you are. Thank you for opening your beautiful heart to see and live more of this gift of life! Infinite Blessings of Love to all!

Printed in the United States
By Bookmasters